Governance for a New Century

The Japan Center for International Exchange wishes to thank

The Nippon Foundation

Japan-U.S. Foundation

Governance for a New Century

Japanese Challenges, American Experience

edited by
Thomas E. Mann and Sasaki Takeshi

JCIE Japan Center for International Exchange
Tokyo ▧ *New York*

The surnames of the authors and other persons mentioned in this book are positioned according to country practice.

Copyediting by Elmer Luke and Pamela J. Noda
Cover and typographic design by Becky Davis, EDS Inc., Editorial & Design Services.
Typesetting and production by EDS Inc.
Cover photograph © 1996 The Studio Dog/PhotoDisc, Inc.

Printed in Japan
ISBN 4-88907-061-3

Distributed outside Japan by Brookings Institution Press (1775 Massachusetts Avenue, N.W., Washington, D.C. 20036-2188 U.S.A.) and Kinokuniya Company Ltd. (5-38-1 Sakuragaoka, Setagaya-ku, Tokyo 156-8691 Japan).

Japan Center for International Exchange
9-17 Minami Azabu 4-chome, Minato-ku, Tokyo 106-0047 Japan
URL: http://www.jcie.or.jp

Japan Center for International Exchange, Inc. (JCIE/USA)
1251 Avenue of the Americas, New York, N.Y. 10020 U.S.A.

Contents

Foreword

Governance for a New Century: Japanese Challenges, American Experience represents the result of a joint study and dialogue project between the Japan Center for International Exchange and the Brookings Institution that was directed by Thomas Mann, W. Averell Harriman Chair and Senior Fellow in Governmental Studies at Brookings, and Sasaki Takeshi, President of the University of Tokyo. The project was launched on the premise that Japan and the United States face many similar challenges of governance, and a comparative study would enable those interested in the improvement of governance in their own society to deepen their understanding of the nature of their respective problems and to learn from each other. Thus, two sets of country papers addressing the same broad issue areas were commissioned from experts in Japan and the United States, and they were discussed at two symposia held in Tokyo on April 7–11, 1999, and Washington, D.C., on March 5–6, 2001.

As this comparative study progressed, it became obvious that Japan was facing a serious crisis of governance with profound implications for its ability to deal with the decade-long economic stagnation and the deteriorating public trust in political processes. The United States, too, is not without its challenges of governance, as the recent Enron scandal underscored. It was felt by those involved in the joint study that a product focused on the Japanese challenges of governance would serve the purpose of improving the quality of debate now raging in Japan and also in the United States in the context of the U.S.-Japan relationship on the future direction of Japan's governance. Accordingly, it was decided that the publication would follow the format of Japanese authors writing on diverse issues of governance related to Japan and relevant reform proposals, and American authors responding on the basis of American experience, including some failures in American reform plans. The chapters contained herein were reported as discussion papers to the Global ThinkNet Tokyo Conference held in Japan in November 2001. Most of the Japanese participants of the project and Thomas Mann attended the conference, and their presentations stimulated a heated debate among other conference participants, including a number of politicians, policy experts from research institutions, journalists, and other public intellectuals.

This volume is a sequel to several publications coming out of a series of projects under the core project theme of "Globalization, Governance, and Civil Society" that JCIE has been pursuing since 1996 in response to a wide array of shifts that had become visible in the mid-1990s in civil society, government, politics, and the interaction between those sectors in the face of formidable forces of globalization. Our first study was an in-depth examination of the role of civil society in the domestic governance of Japan, which resulted in the 1998 *Deciding the Public Good: Governance and Civil Society in Japan.* A subsequent publication entitled *Governance and Civil Society in a Global Age* (2001) sought to build on those findings by introducing an international perspective on the issue of governance and civil society. JCIE has decided to focus on a series of study and dialogue projects focusing on the health of democracies and prospects for improvement in the conduct of politics and the performance of government. In addition to the project resulting in this report, JCIE has published *Guidance for Governance: Comparing Alternative Sources of Public Policy Advice* (2001) and plans to publish the results of a project examining the new policy agenda in Japan and the role of politicians. It is our hope that these publications, which are the result of JCIE's policy study projects under its Global ThinkNet Program, will play a useful role in stimulating constructive debate on the critical issues of governance Japan has to grapple with in the coming years.

I would like to express sincere gratitude to the authors who participated in this long-term project for the serious effort that they put into their analyses and a unique series of dialogues across the Pacific. Special thanks are due to Thomas Mann and Sasaki Takeshi for their serious commitment to this joint study and their insightful leadership throughout the project. This project and the resulting volume would not have been possible without the generous financial support of the Nippon Foundation and the Japan-U.S. Foundation, to which JCIE extends its special thanks. I also would like to recognize the invaluable assistance of JCIE staff who worked on this project at different phases, including Takaku Hiroshi, Bunya Yoshinori, Wada Shūichi, and Suzuki Tomoko. Finally, I wish to thank Pamela J. Noda and Kawaguchi Chie of JCIE for their tireless efforts to ensure that this publication came to fruition.

Yamamoto Tadashi
PRESIDENT
JAPAN CENTER FOR INTERNATIONAL EXCHANGE

Governance for a New Century

1

Overview

Thomas E. Mann and Sasaki Takeshi

THIS volume is one of the fruits of several years of collaboration between the Japan Center for International Exchange and the Brookings Institution exploring the health of our democracies and prospects for improvement in the conduct of politics and government on both sides of the Pacific. The larger project has facilitated useful exchanges in both Japan and the United States involving scholars, politicians, and journalists. These exchanges provided participants an opportunity to learn from one another by focusing on how our two countries have adapted their political institutions to cope with broad forces (the end of the cold war, globalization, demographic shifts, and new communication technologies) and with problems in policy and governance.

Governance for a New Century concerns itself with the volatile period in Japanese politics since the burst of the bubble economy in the early 1990s. The volume features chapters on Japanese public opinion, elections, political finance, party politics, policymaking, and institutional reform contributed by scholars and practitioners in Japan, with responses from American colleagues. We are mindful of Gerald Curtis's admonition that Japan's political system should not be judged by an American standard, and we accept his argument that in many respects Japan is less unique among democracies than is the United States.

3

Nonetheless, we believe American experience can shed some light on the efforts under way in Japan to restructure its electoral and governing processes and to cope with its major policy challenges—just as Japanese experience informs similar efforts in the United States.

REVERSAL OF FORTUNES

At the outset of this project, citizens in both countries saw little they liked about the conduct of politics, but Americans had less reason to disapprove of the performance of their government. After a brief recession at the start, the 1990s proved to be a decade of extraordinary prosperity in the United States, featuring the longest economic expansion in American history. Inflation was contained, productivity surged, real wages increased across all income groups, and federal budget deficits turned into surpluses. At the same time, key social indicators improved: crime, welfare rolls, teenage pregnancy, and abortions all declined. America appeared to be a hotbed of social *rest*.

By contrast, the Japanese public had ample grounds for questioning the effectiveness of their government. After decades of rapid growth and industrial development, Japan entered a very difficult period of asset and price deflation, a stagnant economy, an increasingly fragile banking system, and mounting public debt. While in the 1970s and 1980s Japan appeared to enjoy a strong advantage over the United States in the structure and performance of its political economy—many Americans believed Japan Inc. to be a superior system—the following decade witnessed a striking reversal of fortunes. Now, America—with its robust capital markets, flexible workforce, relatively modest levels of economic regulation, and entrepreneurial values—was seen as well positioned to adapt most successfully to globalization and digital technology.

Public distaste for and disengagement from politics in the United States was a luxury the country found easily affordable. The focus on scandal—highlighted by the impeachment proceedings against President Bill Clinton but a more or less permanent feature of partisan conflict and press attention over the last decade—reflected the absence of more serious challenges to the nation's well-being. Politics in America was so nasty because the stakes were so low. The important work of the country was seen to be getting done in spite of Washington, not because of it.

In contrast, scandals in Japan appeared to be central to flaws in a political system that inhibited effective economic and social responses to the challenges of globalization. Political corruption Japanese-style revealed links among parochial interests, the LDP-dominant and faction-ridden party system, and an intransigent bureaucracy. While demands for political reform intensified in both countries, the sense of urgency in Japan far outstripped that in the United States.

THE CHANGING CONTEXT

This was the context in which we launched our project on governance and political change in Japan and the United States. Who could have imagined the extraordinary developments that would soon unfold in both countries?

In the United States, the 2000 presidential election was the closest in American history, with only several hundred votes in Florida out of more than 100 million ballots cast nationwide determining the winner. After a thirty-six-day political and legal war over the status of mistakenly cast and uncounted Florida ballots, George W. Bush garnered the presidency when, by a 5–4 decision, an ideologically divided Supreme Court ended the manual recount that might have produced a different outcome.

Then on September 11, 2001, nineteen terrorists hijacked four commercial airliners and succeeding in piloting three of them into the World Trade Center towers in New York City and the Pentagon in Washington, D.C., killing more than three thousand American citizens and foreign nationals. If not for the courageous action of passengers, the fourth plane might well have destroyed the U.S. Capitol and members of the Senate and House of Representatives. America was suddenly at war and, as the anthrax attacks in the following weeks made crystal clear, that war would be waged on two fronts—at home and abroad.

The terrorist attack also inflicted a devastating blow to an already anemic American economy, ensuring the first recession in the country since 1991. Growth had slowed in the previous year, and the stock market had lost a substantial part of its value. NASDAQ was especially hard hit, as the high-tech bubble finally burst. With no signs of economic vitality in Europe or Japan, the United States was pulled into the maelstrom of a global economic downturn.

The context of American politics and governance as we end this project is therefore dramatically different from that in which we began. Peace and prosperity were abruptly supplanted by war and recession. Politics as sport gave way to sober reflections on flaws in the election system and the high stakes of leadership selection. The glorification of the private sector dimmed as citizens looked to government as the first line of defense of their physical and economic security. Public trust in government and approval of the president and Congress soared (based, no doubt, more on hope and expectation than performance). Partisan strategies of governance were replaced by the first genuine consultations among party leaders in decades. Governance in America took on a seriousness of purpose not in evidence earlier.

For its part, Japan's political system was rocked by the extraordinary success of Koizumi Jun'ichirō in winning leadership of the Liberal Democratic Party (LDP) in April 2001 after the resignation of Prime Minister Mori Yoshirō and then leading his party to its first major victory in a decade in the House of Councillors election. Koizumi won in spite of (or perhaps because of) opposition from LDP party brokers in the Diet, by building strong support among rank-and-file party members, and by captivating the public with a refreshingly irreverent leadership style. The new prime minister quickly achieved an unprecedented level of popularity, with early job approval ratings reaching 86 percent.

Japan was also affected by the global economic downturn and the terrorist attacks in the United States. The results were less jarring but no less serious than in America. The economic malaise spreading across the globe exacerbated the financial woes long suffered by Japan and complicated the efforts of Koizumi to deal effectively with structural problems without plunging the country further into deflation and recession. The U.S.-led war on terrorism prompted Japan to reinterpret its constitutional prohibition against deploying its Self-Defense Forces beyond its territorial waters.

PERSPECTIVES ON REFORM

What these changes in context portend for politics and governance in Japan and the United States is very difficult to foresee. Our task in this volume is to gauge how the underlying dynamics shaping political change in both countries might be reinforced or altered by these new forces and, as a consequence, what opportunities might be presented or foreclosed for improving politics and governance.

Institutional reform in democratic societies is neither easy to achieve nor fully predictable in its effects. The political histories of Japan and the United States are filled with aborted reform efforts and enacted reforms gone awry. Political energy invested in institutional reform seldom pays clear dividends, especially if the ultimate objective is to remedy policy deficiencies. Some analysts find the "law of unanticipated consequences" associated with political reform so debilitating that they counsel against any major investment in changing the institutional rules of the game. Altering the climate of public opinion, the behavior of voters, the ideas animating policy elites, the quality and independence of policy analysis, the programs and strategies of the political parties, and norms and values within the political community offers, in their view, more productive levers for achieving needed changes in policy.

At the same time, institutions clearly matter. Rules governing elections, representation, government formation and dissolution, bicameralism, federalism, and judicial review, for example, strongly influence the nature of the party system and the policymaking process. Rules and procedures allocating authority and resources within executive and legislative bodies can strengthen or weaken institutional capacity. Institutional arrangements appropriate for one set of conditions and objectives may not be well suited to another. Thus, it would be foolish to ignore institutional arrangements in the quest to improve governmental performance. It would be equally foolish to expect too much of institutional reform—by misreading the conditions that make possible its enactment or by ignoring the complex environment in which reforms are implemented.

American experience recounted in this volume offers both encouragement and pointed cautions for Japanese reformers. Japanese and American contributors both appreciate the extent to which much political change occurs without the passage of major institutional reform. Politicians can precipitate change by recognizing and responding to market signals from the public. Citizens can stimulate change by expressing their dissatisfaction with the performance of the government and their willingness to support an alternative. Economic and security crises can help overcome normal constraints on coalition building and facilitate the enactment of difficult policies. The United States, for example, has had more success in dealing with particular policy problems (such as economic deregulation, the savings and loan crisis, the budget deficits of the 1980s and early 1990s) than in enacting effective political reforms.

Our contributors also recognize that policy mistakes can be made under a wide variety of institutional regimes. Wise policies cannot be guaranteed by getting the institutional rules "just right." Institutional reforms are not panaceas for Japan or the United States, and the reform process itself can become distracting and counterproductive.

The Japanese and American authors of this volume nonetheless endorse a positive but measured approach to political reform, one that does not inflate expectations of what can be achieved quickly, and that takes full account of the linkages among the political dynamics, institutional arrangements, and policymaking capabilities of their respective countries. In Japan, more robust competition among the parties for control of government, an electorate sufficiently informed and exercised to hold its elected leaders accountable, and a prime minister with the resolve and resources to provide effective leadership are essential if substantial progress is to be made on a very challenging policy agenda.

SUMMARY

Yoshida Shin'ichi opens the volume with a broad overview of what he describes as a revolutionary period in Japanese politics. The lingering recession following the collapse of the bubble economy generated increasing frustration in the public, eventually building to widespread anger and distrust of politicians, political parties, and the Japanese way of governing. Yoshida places particular importance on the rise in the number of voters who identify with no political party. These nonaffiliated voters have introduced an element of uncertainty and fluidity into elections, with huge vote swings in response to news events and campaign appeals. The public base of support for the long-dominant LDP collapsed, leading to a breakdown in the party's rural constituency–based political machine, a defection of LDP Diet members to new parties, and an ongoing scramble to forge coalitions with smaller parties to maintain power.

Koizumi's stunning success in grasping the reins of the LDP and leading his party to a decisive victory in the House of Councillors election reflected LDP weakness, not strength. Koizumi won for the LDP by running against the LDP. Yoshida argues that public demands for accountability and responsiveness have already weakened the bureaucratic structure of Japanese government and society, created a market for more assertive political leadership, and begun to alter patterns of public spending. Voters have launched a process that will eventually transform politics and governance in Japan.

E. J. Dionne Jr. agrees with Yoshida that voter discontent is at the root of many changes in Japanese politics, as it has been in the United States and many other democracies. But he wonders whether any set of political reforms and new leadership styles can temper that discontent if there is no noticeable improvement in economic performance. Japan's imperfectly developed party system, Dionne argues, has contributed substantially to voters' frustration with the political process. Moving toward a system of two major parties or blocs would provide a more direct means of holding governments accountable and replacing those in power. But Japan has made only halting progress in this regard, as the two major parties, the Liberal Democratic Party and the Democratic Party of Japan, have not yet found their distinct ideological space. The old system collapsed primarily because it no longer delivered economic prosperity. That ultimately made possible the emergence of Koizumi and a new politics. Now Koizumi has to return Japan to economic health, and quickly, if that new politics is to survive and flourish.

Katō Hideki tracks the 130-year transformation of Japan from a traditional society of self-reliant communities into one best characterized as a "state monopoly on public affairs." Advanced in the Meiji era (1868–1912) as a strategy to catch up with Western societies and then largely repeated after the devastating setbacks of World War II, the design was one in which the government dominated decisions as to what constituted the public interest as well as the mechanisms established to serve that public interest. Katō demonstrates how this state monopoly has been institutionalized through Article 34 of the Civil Code, which gives public authorities the responsibility for deciding the standards under which public interest groups may apply for official standing, and the establishment laws of the central government ministries and agencies, which provide for the sweeping exercise of administrative guidance by bureaucrats. When combined with other administrative arrangements such as central government subsidies and revenue sharing for local governments, Katō notes, these provisions put virtually every aspect of national life in Japan under the purview of the government.

Katō recommends a series of steps to help develop a vibrant civil society that encourages citizens to define and implement important aspects of public affairs apart from the "competent authorities" of the central government. These include the establishment of independent committees in the prefectures to judge the qualifications of nonprofit organizations' activities for tax-favored treatment, the repeal of establishment laws that confer broad discretionary authority on bureaucrats, and a decentralization of public finance.

Paul Light is struck by the similarity between Japan and the United States in the sheer velocity of administrative reform. Noting Katō's observation that Japan has been buffeted by a series of reforms undertaken on an ad hoc basis to deal with widely publicized problems, he believes Japan may be suffering from the American disease of too much reform rather than too little. Light reviews four tides of administrative reform in the United States—scientific management, liberation management, watchful eye, and war on waste—and shows where each has surfaced in the reform debate in Japan. By discussing a number of problems that developed in the United States when the tides collided, Light provides a cautionary note to those who would accelerate the pace of reform without giving each element sufficient time to take hold. This advice appears consistent with Katō's view that previous rounds of administrative reform have been largely ineffectual, and that a more fundamental diagnosis of the problem and a more tailored approach to reform are required.

Shiozaki Yasuhisa draws on his experience as a member of the Japanese parliament—in particular his involvement with a group of junior but substantively knowledgeable politicians in enacting the Financial Revitalization Law of 1998—to describe the ways in which the policy process is adapting to the collapse of the old iron-triangle system. Shiozaki chronicles the political instability of the "lost decade" of the 1990s and the harmful swings in policy associated with it. A largely ad hoc policy process has struggled to provide direction and coherence in the absence of a beacon, or control tower, in government. Small groups of politicians, with the encouragement of one or two party leaders, have sought to develop a policy capacity independent of the traditionally dominant bureaucracy. But the steps taken to date have been inadequate to deal with the major policy challenges confronting Japan. Shiozaki recommends a number of measures to strengthen the independent lawmaking capacity of the Diet, including year-round sessions, additional political appointments to the staffs of the prime minister and members of his cabinet, and greater transparency in the policy process.

As different as the Japanese and American political systems and cultures are, James Lindsay notes the striking familiarity of the story told by Shiozaki. Lindsay, a student of the U.S. Congress, reminds us that until the 1970s, decision making in Congress was relatively centralized, with powerful committees and senior members playing a dominant role. In this setting, iron triangles brought together committees, federal agencies, and interest groups into alliances of mutual cooperation, much like the old pattern in Japan described by Shiozaki. Driven by external and internal pressures, the winds of reform swept through Congress in the 1970s, leading to a decentralization of power and major expansion of congressional staff—in members' offices, in committees, and in agencies providing policy analysis for the entire Congress. Congress became a more democratic institution, more responsive to public sentiment, and much better equipped to analyze policy proposals independent of the executive. Yet it has become even more difficult to pass major pieces of legislation, as narrow interests find enhanced access to legislators and increased opportunities for hostage taking. Indeed, in recent years congressional reformers have sought some recentralization of power. Lindsay concedes some democratization and capacity building may be needed in the Diet, but he cautions that these reforms will almost certainly prove to be double-edged swords.

Money plays a prominent and problematic role in elections and policymaking in both Japan and the United States. The next chapter in this volume features an analysis of political funding law and practice in Japan. Taniguchi Masaki's review of the history of political funding reform in Japan reveals more success in changing the law than in producing the desired effects. The problem, he argues, is that a candidate-centered electoral system generates tremendous pressure on politicians to raise large amounts of money. Without reduction in the demand for political funds, legal restraints on fundraising will be circumvented by ambitious politicians, either by creative maneuvers around or corrupt violations of the law.

Taniguchi demonstrates how loophole-ridden laws have gradually been strengthened, especially in the area of disclosure and enforcement. But even here the system in Japan appears to be designed to control information, not to disseminate it to the public on a timely basis. Public funding of political parties has somewhat diminished the scramble for funds and reduced the reliance on contributions from companies. Taniguchi argues that the Japanese "soft money" problem should be the focus of the next round of funding reform. A prohibition on company donations to politicians is being circumvented by the proliferation of local party branches entirely beholden to individual politicians. This weakens accountability and ultimately the legitimacy of the system.

Thomas Mann observes that American experience since the passage of the landmark U.S. federal campaign finance law in 1974 substantiates Taniguchi's argument that attempts to limit the supply of political funds without reducing demand are bound to generate pressures that eventually undermine those limits. In both countries, the distance between the stated intentions of reformers and the actual consequences of the law has been great. But Mann, like Taniguchi, does not conclude that all funding reform is doomed to failure. Instead, solutions are necessarily partial and temporary, and provide limited leverage on broader problems of governance. Political funding problems cannot be solved in any decisive and permanent sense; they must be managed in ways that do not do violence to other values that each country holds dear. From this perspective, Mann discusses the political finance tools available to policymakers—disclosure, contribution limits, spending limits, public subsidies, and regulation of campaign activity—and draws lessons for Japan from American experience with each of them.

The volume concludes with an essay by Sasaki Takeshi on the linkages between party politics and governance in Japan and a response by Kent Weaver on the limits of institutional reform. Sasaki analyzes the shifts in public support for the parties between the Diet elections of 1996 and 2000, detecting the emergence of more distinct social cleavages and a loss of confidence in the ability of LDP-style governance to deal with the structural economic crisis. Rapid turnover in the prime minister's office (eight prime ministers in the 1990s) and constant reshuffling of the cabinet destroyed the preconditions for strong political leadership. Pressure developed to shift from a bureaucracy-dominated to a politics-dominated system, with the latter characterized by a Japanese-style political appointee system in the prime minister's office and in the ministries. But this new system is frustrated by the continuing appeal within the LDP for the old-style exchange games between politicians and bureaucrats.

Sasaki describes an ambitious agenda of reform of society and governance, built around the core values of deregulation and decentralization, and detailed in *The Frontier Within: Individual Empowerment and Better Governance in the New Millenium,* the report of the Prime Minister's Commission on Japan's Goals in the 21st Century. The critical question, he asks, is what kind of pressures can bring about real change in the postwar system. Many politicians and members of the public have been attracted to the idea of the direct election of the prime minister as a way of strengthening political leadership. But Sasaki notes the uncertainty of whether this proposal would strengthen the prime minister within his own party, where he has been noticeably weak.

Kent Weaver weighs in decisively against the direct election of the prime minister. Drawing on Israel's unhappy experience with this reform, he concludes direct election is very unlikely to strengthen the prime minister, to consolidate support in the two major parties, or to make him less subject to constant threats from small parties in his coalition. Weaver believes the consequences of direct election would be even more disappointing to proponents than was the 1994 electoral reform that replaced the single non-transferable vote (SNTV) system with a mixed-member majoritarian (MMM) system. He reminds us that institutional reforms do not appear on a blank slate, but interact with a set of institutions and interests that are already well entrenched. Instead, Weaver suggests a series of more moderate reforms to strengthen the prime minister within his own party and to make it somewhat easier for governments to impose policies that cause short-term pain but have some promise of long-term gain. He also cautions against further reform of the electoral system, which would be seen (correctly) by the public as manipulation by elites for political gain.

2

Distrust of Politics: Will Voters Transform the Nature of Governance?

Yoshida Shin'ichi

WITHIN the past decade, various developments that had been until now unthinkable have taken place in politics and governance in Japan. In 1993, the Liberal Democratic Party (LDP) lost its single-party grip on power and was forced to collaborate with other parties in order to stay in power. As a result, political parties were forced to reexamine their perspective and their sense of direction for the nation. The various coalition governments entered into uncharted territory. All this has led to significant changes in the power once enjoyed by bureaucrats and the structure that has governed them.

These developments, however, do not mean that the system of government in Japan has changed. What has changed is the underpinnings of the system—the political parties, the bureaucracy, and other subsystems. And this is an indication that Japanese politics and administration—put broadly, the quality of governance—are beginning to change.

Another decade or two will be needed before we can see how these developments have left their mark. At this point, it is clear only that the changes did not take place gradually. What caused them was the demand of the times—a lingering, unprecedented recession that Japan has been enduring since the collapse of the bubble economy of the 1980s. The society felt stuck, unable to move on. Frustration led to anxiety and anger. In other words, distrust of politics. It is this distrust that has prompted changes in the political process and the media as well. It has rocked the political establishment. It is dismantling conventional ways of governing.

What is sought is a new politics, an escape from the inertia that has prevailed. Perhaps I overstate my case, but I believe the past decade has been a revolutionary period where unprecedented demands from voters have led to dramatic changes in the way this nation is governed.

In summer 2001, under Prime Minister Koizumi Jun'ichirō, the LDP scored its first major victory in ten years in the House of Councillors election. Support for the prime minister has remained strong since, and the media suggest that the LDP has regained power and popularity. Whether true or not, of more fundamental importance is the message sent by the voters in this election.

Koizumi was swept into power because of the desire among voters for change in politics. The victory of the Koizumi-led LDP was an indication that voters were willing to trust an LDP that pledged to deny its past and to change. Indeed, the changes in the past decade have transformed politics and governance in Japan to such a degree that it is impossible to expect a resurgence of the old-style rule by the LDP.

Non-Party Affiliation and Fluid Voter Support

VOTERS WITH NO PARTY AFFILIATION

One of the biggest political changes in the last decade has been the emergence of a huge bloc of voters who claimed to endorse no political party.

After enjoying many years in power, the LDP in the early 1990s entered a period of intra-party strife stemming from battles between the various factions. This bickering eventually split the party and ended the LDP's one-party rule over the country. These changes coincided with changes in the economic and social fabric of Japan as the asset-inflated bubble collapsed and the economy continued to globalize. These factors created an environment where conventional policies no longer worked. Thus, after the LDP split, Japanese politics entered a period of confusion where lawmakers struggled to find new political visions and ways to achieve them.

New political parties emerged. While it was unclear where the

nation was heading politically, the
Japanese economy stagnated further. Not unexpectedly, voter frustration rose. Opinion polls showed
an unprecedented 70 percent to
80 percent of voters dissatisfied
with politics. This distrust translated into declines in voter turnout and indifference to political
activity in general. Support for the
LDP and other mainstream parties fell at the same time that the
number of voters who endorsed
no political party rose (table 1).

Table 1. LDP Supporters versus Voters with
No Party Affiliation (%)

Year	LDP	Nonaffilated
1990	47	29
1991	49	31
1992	36	42
1993	23	45
1994	24	50
1995	28	46
1996	31	44
1997	30	52
1998	27	48
1999	34	43
2000	28	50
2001	39	37

Source: Asahi Shimbun, from data compiled yearly
in December based on polls conducted quarterly.
Data for 2001 are through August.

Support for the LDP was highest in 1991, but the following year
saw nonaffiliated voters outnum-
bering LDP supporters for the first time. What table 1 does not show is
that, in some periods during the past ten years, nonaffiliated voters even
exceeded 60 percent.

FLUIDITY AND "WIND"

Nonaffiliated voters have several characteristics. Research conducted
by the *Asahi Shimbun* found that, in the period 1993–1996, among voters
classified as without party affiliation, 70 percent had endorsed a political party. A 1999 survey by the *Asahi Shimbun* had similar findings, with
a little over 60 percent of nonaffiliated voters having endorsed a political
party in national elections within the previous three years. Thus, nonaffiliated voters do not necessarily mean voters who do not support
political parties at all. Rather, they are voters who will frequently shift
their support among various political parties, depending on the circumstances.

At the same time, voters who do support a particular political party
appear to be changing their allegiances more often. According to a 1995
study, only 20 percent to 30 percent of voters with a party affiliation indicated they had continuously supported that party over the previous
year. Together with the rising number of nonaffiliated voters, this finding would suggest that a large mass of voters no longer feel that support

for a certain political party is binding. These are the "fluid" or "floating" voters.

It should be noted that a conspicuously large number of voters who had no strong party affiliation during the 1990s still maintained a keen interest in politics. This new breed of nonaffiliated voters, in contrast to nonaffiliated voters of the past who were indifferent to politics, keeps abreast of political events through newspapers and television. In a way, then, they may have been disillusioned and seeking a party to support but were unsuccessful at finding one. These nonaffiliated voters tend to respond quickly to the mood of the times, the swings of which are reflected in their voting patterns. This phenomenon has come to be called the "wind" of nonaffiliated voters.

The first such wind blew in 1995 when voters in Tokyo and Osaka, the country's two largest cities, elected as their governors candidates who were comedians and who ran without the backing of any political party. In national elections for the House of Councillors in 1995 and 1998 and the House of Representatives in 2000, the results were similarly affected by the wind of nonaffiliated voters. The June 2000 general election saw the unexpected rise of the Democratic Party of Japan (DPJ), which one survey found 30 percent of nonaffiliated voters to have supported.

The wind picked up speed as politicians depended more on the mass media to communicate their message. From the politically chaotic early 1990s, political talk shows and news programs started to have a strong influence on voters as well, and the government of Prime Minister Hosokawa Morihiro is said to have come into being from an anti-LDP mood generated by such television programs. Broadcasters have used dramatic political developments as fodder for new programs, which drives public sentiment further. The same can be said of tabloid shows on television when they pick up political topics. In Japan, as elsewhere, "tele-politics" has sped up the dissemination of political news, generating support or opposition almost instantly. This has pushed Japanese politics into a more volatile period.

The easily changeable wind has sharply reduced the ability of pollsters and lawmakers to predict the response of the public or the outcome of elections. While Japanese media organizations have developed what they say are scientific methods for predicting public opinion based on data of voter patterns and opinion polls, since 1995, however, there have been many instances where their predictions have been completely wrong. Predicting voter turnout and voter reaction has also become increasingly difficult. One example is during the 1998 House of Councillors election, in which the media expected that the LDP would win more than 60 seats; it won just over 40 seats, resulting in a dramatic defeat for the party.

THE KOIZUMI PHENOMENON

The Koizumi phenomenon that has dominated Japanese politics since spring 2001 is a direct result of a more fluid voter sentiment driven by the media.

In the LDP presidential election in April, general voters were drawn to Koizumi, who came across to the public as an independent politician within the party. The public was impressed by his pledge to bravely implement political and economic reforms. Koizumi generated a sense of urgency among voters by making it clear that unless he was elected as LDP president, the future of the LDP would be uncertain. This in turn helped Koizumi, who had little support within the party, to create a sense within the party that it was necessary he be elected.

Koizumi's populism did not stop there. As the head of the ruling LDP, Koizumi took over as prime minister. After setting up his administration, he skillfully used the media to get his points across, and as a result, his cabinet has consistently maintained an unusually high support rating of around 80 percent. Against this backdrop, a huge mass of nonaffiliated voters shifted their support to the LDP.

Thanks to the strong support for the Koizumi cabinet, the LDP scored a major victory in the July 2001 election for the House of Councillors, winning a majority of the contested seats for the first time in nine years. Koizumi's popularity has continued. A survey by the *Asahi Shimbun* in August 2001 showed that support for the LDP had increased since the election, while the percentage of nonaffiliated voters had declined. For the first time since 1992, LDP supporters outnumbered nonaffiliated voters, suggesting a return of power to the LDP (see table 1).

Koizumi's popularity has indeed moved nonaffiliated voters. Exit polls during the House of Councillors election showed that nonaffiliated votes for the LDP nearly tripled in comparison to the election three years before. This rise in support for the LDP was *not* attributed to former LDP supporters coming back to the party. It is premature to suggest that the LDP has regained voter confidence because there is no guarantee that fluid voters will stay with the LDP. Opinion polls before the July 2001 House of Councillors election showed that 70 percent of nonaffiliated voters supported Koizumi. But among these Koizumi supporters, there were more who wanted to see the opposition DPJ take power than who wanted the LDP to lead. Another point worth noting is that more than half the supporters of the Japanese Communist Party (JCP) back Koizumi. Thus, it appears that Koizumi is supported by voters who would promptly ditch the LDP if they became dissatisfied with the course of politics and governance.

Simply put, Koizumi's popularity stems from the anti-LDP sentiment that characterized the distrust of politics during the 1990s. This point should not be overlooked. Koizumi never hesitated to say publicly that he would break up the LDP if he had to. The bold decisiveness of this statement helped to attract many fluid voters. In this sense, the Koizumi phenomenon was brought on by swings in voter support, something that has grown over the past decade. How this trend will evolve is uncertain.

In the age of tele-politics, mass media play a large role. But voters, as consumers of mass media, are often fickle. Nonaffiliated voters in Tokyo, for example, viewed comedian Aoshima Yukio as a hero and elected him governor in 1995. But Aoshima could not sustain that momentum and did not even run for a second term. Is the Koizumi phenomenon solid enough to allow him to build a stable Koizumi era? The answer to this question will perhaps be seen in the not-so-distant future.

The Dynamics of Distrust

THE QUALITY OF POLITICS

It was distrust of politics that caused instability in Japanese politics and fluidity of voter support. What was the nature of this distrust? What is the message of this distrust?

In the 1990s, distrust of politicians and political systems was brewing not only in Japan but also in Europe and the United States. In other countries, the issue was more about voter isolation from the political process. The degree of distrust in Japan, however, is higher than in other countries, and the type of distrust is comparably peculiar in Japan.

Figures 1 and 2 show results of polls conducted by the *Asahi Shimbun*

Figure 1. "Do you believe that your vote counts?"

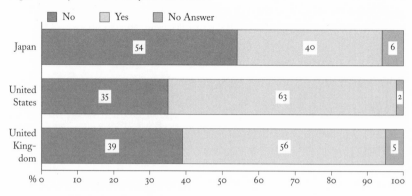

Source: Asahi Shimbun 29 December 1998.

Figure 2. "How would you characterize the number of politicians who are dishonest? (many, some, none)"

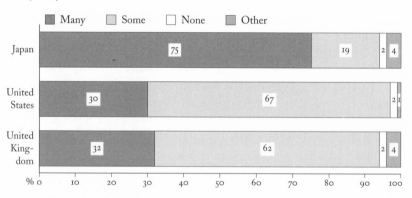

Source: Asahi Shimbun 29 December 1998.

to gauge the trust in politics of voters in the United States, the United Kingdom, and Japan. What distinguishes Japan from the other two countries is the particularly strong sense of voter cynicism and power-lessness. In response to the question, "Do you believe that your vote counts?" an overwhelming majority of U.S. and U.K. voters said yes; in Japan, an overwhelming majority said no. In response to a question to gauge the quantity of politicians that voters believed were engaged in dishonest acts, in Japan a staggering 75 percent answered "many"—more than twice the number who answered similarly in the United States and the United Kingdom. In all three countries, politicians are often the butt of jokes, "the bad guys," but voters in Japan see their politicians as more untrustworthy than do voters in other countries.

The results of this poll are telling and alarming both. Such strong distrust does not come from voters' feeling isolated, but rather from voters' being shut out for so long and harboring no hope of being involved in the political process in the future. As has been borne out by research as well as election results, this deep distrust cannot be healed through mere technical reforms that aim to include voters in the ballot box. Healing can only result through bold reforms that change the quality of politics in Japan.

Yet, what are the roots of this discontent? While there are no data to draw from, we might offer these possible explanations. One is the conventional view: politics and governance have nothing to do with voters and are done by someone else somewhere else. This sense of remotness from government may have emerged in postwar Japan as voters came to undertstand that one vote does not always mean one vote. Rather, the weight of one vote can differ sharply, depending on constitutency and geography—an imbalance that has been long left unaddressed.

Another is the fair possibility that voters may be finally waking up politically, with the reality that Japan's affluent society, which was created almost in inertia after World War II, now faces a crisis. But whatever the explanation, what is clear is that public distrust in politics first emerged in the form of voters' shunning established parties—in particular, the governing LDP.

THE LDP IN A CORNER

Even after the confusion during the 1990s, the LDP still appears to believe it is the champion of Japanese politics. But there are many concerns it faces: the fluidity of voters, which dismantled the party's support base, and the fact that the pork barrel cannot be counted on to bring in the votes.

In fact, the decade witnessed the party rapidly losing its grip. In the proportional representation section of the House of Councillors elections in 1995 and 1998, voters deserted the LDP en masse. Only one in seven or eight voters, including those who abstained, cast ballots for the LDP. The ruling party came to a crisis of losing its legitimacy.

The decline was so sharp that the party could not arrest it with technical tactics, try though it did. In 1996, the government introduced a single-seat constituency system (to be combined with a bloc of seats chosen by proportional representation) in the House of Representatives election. This was a system that from its inception favored the ruling party, but the tactic was to no avail. In the 1996 election, support for the LDP fell further, and the party was met with strong competition from the opposition New Frontier Party (Shinshintō). LDP members expressed concern that the single-seat constituency system would in fact undermine the LDP if the number of fluid voters increased further.

Worse yet, the rising tide of nonaffiliated voters proved to be basically anti-LDP, as indicated before. After 1995, whenever there was a large turnout of nonaffiliated voters, the LDP lost badly. This was the obverse of what the LDP had been used to. Previously, if the LDP mobilized voters and boosted voter turnout, the LDP could expect to win. But by the mid-1990s, the LDP started to realize that the lower the voter turnout, the better the party did.

A good example of this was the House of Councillors election in 1998. The LDP calculated that it could win if it mobilized what was left of its support base, provided that voter turnout was low. It was an attempt to preserve the old political system using old political techniques. Election day, however, saw a huge number of nonaffiliated voters flocking to polling stations and casting their ballots for the DPJ. The LDP suffered a historic loss.

THE ONGOING REVOLT

The LDP persevered, but so did voters. As they shunned the LDP, they were sending this message to politicians: "Political parties are not important; what is important is what politics can be delivered." Essentially, voters wanted a new political system. The message became abundantly clear in the local gubernatorial elections in 1995.

As stated earlier, the elections in Tokyo and Osaka were the debut of the nonaffiliated voter. Elected as the governors of Japan's two largest cities were two comedians, each without the backing of a party. In the 1999 election for the governor of Tokyo, Ishihara Shintarō was the winner, drawing support from nonaffiliated voters and defeating candidates backed by the LDP and the DPJ. After Ishihara was elected, he was moved to say: "People think the current political parties have almost no value. Ironically, those political parties are unaware of it."

The number of voter revolts has increased as the chasm between

voters and political parties widens: In fall 2000, Tanaka Yasuo, a writer
without political background, ran as an outsider for the governorship of
Nagano Prefecture. For forty years, former officials from the prefectural
government had held this post, but local businesses and private citizens
backed Tanaka and an overwhelming number of nonaffiliated voters
climbed on board the bandwagon. Tanaka won, attacking the political
machine that tried to lure votes by promising public works contracts.

In Tochigi Prefecture, a political novice claiming to represent the ordinary citizen on the street beat the incumbent governor running for
his fifth term.

In March 2001, in Chiba Prefecture, nonaffiliated civic and volunteer
groups threw their support behind a female candidate who promised to
work for environmental preservation and quality-of-life issues. She beat
out a candidate supported by political parties, including the LDP, to
become the first female governor of the prefecture.

With just months to go before the national House of Councillors
election, the upset in Chiba tolled a bell within the LDP. So grave was
the sense of this crisis that the country saw the sudden emergence of
Koizumi and his rise to the prime ministership.

Of course, the election in Chiba Prefecture was not the first time the
LDP had seen the growing demand for new politics. During the past
ten years, there have been occasional calls for an overhaul of politics.
The first such call may have been the formation of a new party in 1993
by a splinter group from the LDP. In fact, each time it loses an election,
the LDP has a heated discussion on how to reform the party. "Unless
we include civic energy such as nonprofit organizations in the party,
there will be no rebirth of true conservative politics," Katō Kōichi, former secretary-general of the LDP, once said.

As this remark indicates, the LDP leadership was already well aware
of the need for change. Yet, the soul searching never led to any major action, and any attempt to change the party was smothered by the com-
placency and inertia of several decades. In fall 2000, Katō, who led a
faction advocating reform within the party, started a revolt against then
Prime Minister Mori. Although Katō had the support of many nonaffiliated voters, his move to split from the party was quelled. Koizumi
was behind the move to silence Katō's rebellion. It was not until Koizumi, the man who helped thwart Katō's rebellion, took center stage
that calls for specific action to reform politics became an official issue in
the LDP.

The "New Politics"

ACCOUNTABILITY AND RESPONSIVENESS

What in essence are nonaffiliated voters after when they seek a "new politics"? This is a difficult question to answer. Nonaffiliated voters are often described by what they are anti-: anti-LDP, anti-incumbent, wanting an anti-establishment party. Accordingly, it is difficult to pinpoint what they are for; yet, looking at the issues they are repeatedly negative about should offer some clues.

If we consider the turbulent changes to the confusion-filled process of policy formulation during the past ten years, we observe many attempts to acquire two new qualities. One is accountability, and the other is responsiveness. These two qualities have emerged as key concepts every time Japanese politics has reached a crucial juncture.

The Japanese phrase *leaving matters up to the superior* captures the traditional view of politics, shared by many, that politics in Japan belongs to those in power. Democracy, introduced to Japan upon the end of World War II, is somewhat antithetical to this concept, however. The essential theory behind democracy is that political authority is accorded to those who win a mandate from voters. Put another way, what politicians in Japan seem not to grasp is that in order to govern effectively in a democratic society, politicians must have a sustained understanding of what the governed want. So they often do not respond to what voters have to say.

One reason for this may be that in Japan the concept for accountability does not exist, as has often been pointed out by Japan specialists in Europe and the United States. Instead of accountability, the Japanese postwar political process has been concerned with determining how to share the fruits of economic growth. Such a process was well met by the old way of politics, but those fruits began to shrivel about the time Japanese society began to turn gray. Politicians thus can no longer talk about the future without explaining the greater burden and pain that society must bear.

In the mid-1990s, there was a period when accountability became the buzzword in Japanese politics, used with regard to government intervention in the liquidation of nonperforming loans held by housing loan corporations. The word stressed the overlooked rights and feelings of taxpayers. It was used frequently in the media, was translated into Japanese, and was even widely referred to in official government documents.

Accountability was not limited to housing loan corporations. After that it came up frequently, and in the late 1990s led to an information disclosure act and the establishment of a law governing the ethical conduct of public servants. The importance of accountability has loomed so large that politicians cannot now ignore it. When the LDP suffered an unexpected setback in the 1998 House of Councillors election, politicians concluded that it was the issue of accountability that turned voters against them, ascribing the defeat to their inability to fully account for the needs of voters.

If accountability means keeping information flowing to voters, responsiveness means receiving feedback from voters and listening to their demands. These days, politicians discuss the need for responsiveness all the time, regardless of whether they are in the government or the opposition. Such discussion has focused on party reform and election strategy. As discussed earlier, since the 1990s tele-politics has increased the pressure on politicians to be ever more responsive.

In the past, the lack of responsiveness was highlighted in public debate at a meeting of LDP executives after defeat in the 2000 general election. Candidates were criticized for their lack of responsiveness and the party for its inability to address voter needs. Yamasaki Taku, the current secretary-general of the party, declared: "The LDP should seriously listen to the voice of the nation, which sees the LDP serving its purpose in the twentieth century." Junior members, meanwhile, went so far as to say that if matters were left unattended, the LDP would destroy itself; as it was, half the voters believed the LDP to be a thing of the past, incapable of meeting challenges in a new age. They lamented the fact that the LDP was too shielded from voters.

But whether it is accountability or responsiveness, each is essential to democracy because it offers a venue for continuing dialogue with voters. The lack, or inadequacy, of accountability or responsiveness has seen its consequences in the long, sharp decline in voter turnout. By the time Japan entered the 1990s, this was clear. Yet, the governing party needed ten years to figure it out—a symptom of the inertia that has plagued Japanese politics under many years of one-party rule.

GOVERNANCE IN TRANSFORMATION

Is Japanese society changing? Or has it changed as a result of the incorporation of elements of accountability and responsiveness?

As stated at the outset, the calls for change have been loud, though the total picture has been hard to see. Yet, the results of gubernatorial elections and certain shifts in central government policy give us hope. As contact between politicians and voters improves, defective aspects of Japanese governance start to crumble. One such feature is the "bureaucratic" society.

Under the name of maintaining continuity, a number of career bureaucrats have long controlled information and written the policy of government. They have manipulated politicians and policy. Whereas politicians were viewed as power seekers interested in private interests, bureaucrats enjoyed the image of fair, neutral administrators (an image consistent with the tendency to view the public sector highly but to look down on the private sector). In this sense, Japan has been led by bureaucrats accorded a superior position in society.

But starting in the 1980s, it became evident that bureaucrats were seeking to maintain continuity of the status quo rather than pushing for necessary economic and social reform. Public awareness was helped by scandals involving bureaucrats at the Ministry of Health and Welfare, the Ministry of Finance, the Ministry of Foreign Affairs, and other agencies. The distrust of politics of the 1990s emerged against the backdrop of a dysfunctional bureaucracy. There was also a sense that the public wanted not bureaucratic leadership but political leadership. This has increased expectations for societal restructuring centered on the private sector.

It has accelerated the dismantling of a bureaucratic society. During a 1998 Diet session to discuss ways to weather a financial crisis, politicians relied on private-sector experts in formulating policies for parliament; this was in contrast to the usual session where bureaucrats prepared policies. The young politicians particularly keen on drafting their own bills were called *seisaku shinjinrui* (a new breed of policymakers). In 2001, after many years of debate, several central government offices were finally merged, creating less bulky organizations. All of this was a challenge for bureaucrats dependent on vested interests surrounding the old structure.

In this atmosphere of a society moving beyond its reliance on the bureaucracy, the Koizumi administration emerged. This sense of the times has helped him to maintain very high support ratings. In May 2001, a district court found the government was liable for damages to leprosy patients who had been treated unfairly for many years through social segregation. As they had in similar lawsuits against the government, bureaucrats insisted on appealing the ruling, but Koizumi did the un-expected: he opposed the bureaucrats, and he acknowledged the re-sponsibility of the government. This drew applause from the public, which saw Koizumi as an individual with both honor and authority.

Koizumi is also challenging the power of the bureaucrats who have cultivated vested interests linked to government-affiliated organizations and public corporations. As his reform programs involve, among other things, privatization of these organizations, Koizumi is attacking the backbone of the bureaucracy. A society characterized by the supremacy of bureaucrats is thus being transformed into a society where the power of bureaucrats has been put more properly in its place.

Changes in Japanese society will not be limited to the bureaucrats. Not only is the structure of governance built around centralized author-ity crumbling, but there also have been rapid shifts in policy with regard to public works, which had been used to feed the LDP political machine and traditional links among politicians, bureaucrats, and businesses. As distrust of politics rose in the 1990s, the LDP first attempted to guard public spending and to weather the difficulty with the conventional pork barrel. How can one forget the 1996 statement of LDP leader Kamei Shizuka, who was later to become the construction minister: "We will not allocate public works projects to those constituencies that will not cast ballots for LDP candidates." The lesson was to be learned the hard way: the LDP lost the 1998 House of Councillors election and was ef-fectively defeated in the 2000 general election.

"Politics that provides benefits to only a limited number of groups will not last," Koizumi has stated unequivocally. Under his adminis-tration, there have been open debate and fundamental reviews of public works projects.

BEYOND COMMON SENSE

With these dramatic changes, the state of Japanese governance is en-tering a completely different world. One of the forces that brought this about is, without a doubt, voter distrust.

The distrust generated a tension both in politics and society. As a re-sult, there was transformation. Politicians have begun to communicate directly with voters, to hear their voices, and to respond—all of which activities are essential to the dynamism of democracy.

This transformation has occurred even as, in the 1980s, revisionist views of Japanese society from abroad suggested that Japan was incapable of reforming itself because it functioned under different principles from those of Europe and the United States and that foreign pressure was therefore necessary. This argument found many even in Japan who would agree that Japanese society has been stubborn. Yet, if the changes described here are any indication, Japan is by itself beginning to find the solutions needed for it to move forward.

3

Why Does the Wind Blow?
The Economy and the Future of
Japanese Political Reform

E. J. Dionne Jr.

THE history of democracies suggests that voters will tolerate a good deal of inefficiency, mismanagement, arrogance, and even corruption if their political systems deliver them tangible benefits, especially of the economic sort.

And so the question for Japanese democracy is whether the "revolutionary period" Yoshida Shin'ichi describes so well in his chapter would have occurred absent the collapse of the bubble economy and the downturn of the 1990s.

The issue is of more than hypothetical or historical interest. The future of Japanese politics depends greatly on whether the demand for change so evident in election after election has been driven primarily by economic discontent or by the social changes Yoshida documents. If the answer lies mostly in economics, then the success of Prime Minister Koizumi Jun'ichirō's experiment will depend less on his obvious command of public relations and the public mood than on his ability to turn around the performance of the Japanese economy.

If true, this would mean that Koizumi may not be the master of his own fate, since economic success depends in significant part on global factors beyond the control of Japan or indeed any nation. Reforms and new departures, however welcomed by Japan's citizens, will be judged not by their intentions or even by their capacity to create a more open society, but by the exacting measures of the unemployment rate, income, and assets.

But is a purely economic explanation of Japan's political malaise sufficient? After all, the distrust Yoshida discusses has many other sources. The demand for accountability reflected a broad and steady democratization of Japanese society that was not matched by a democratization of politics. If economic failure was the trigger for the popular revolt against the Japanese political establishment, many who joined it were also angered by corruption and by the widening gap between the old bureaucratic culture and a public that was increasingly impatient with rigidity. There was also frustration at the seeming intractability of the political system. No matter how the Japanese voted, the system seemed to stay the same. No wonder so few Japanese voters believed that their vote had power.

As a result, one cannot underestimate the importance of the country's imperfectly developed party system in fostering discontent. For decades, there was no effective alternative government to the one formed by the Liberal Democratic Party (LDP). For various reasons, some of them related to the cold war, many Japanese voters were not willing to risk the election of a government dominated by the Socialist Party—let alone a coalition that might include the country's once-important Japanese Communist Party. In this sense, as many scholars and journalists have noted, Japanese politics closely resembled Italian politics. For more than three decades after World War II, the Italian Christian Democrats dominated government because a crucial bloc of voters were unwilling to see the Italian Communist Party as an alternative government. Only with the end of the cold war did the Italian system begin to transform itself into a two-bloc, if not exactly a two-party, system. This led to hope that Japan, too, would move in this direction.

The failure of the Japanese party system is underscored by the exceptionally large number of voters who switched their LDP allegiances not to another party but to no affiliation. As Yoshida notes, the non-affiliated became the single largest bloc of voters and at times reached 60 percent of the electorate.

It is worth noting both where this development parallels political changes in the United States and where it does not. Over a comparable period, the United States, too, saw the growth in the number of self-described independents and even, on occasion, the rise of independent political figures, Ross Perot and the professional wrestler Jesse Ventura being the most famous. (If protesting Japanese voters elected comedians as governors, Minnesota's voters were not far behind in their choice of Ventura.) Some of the same forces of political alienation Yoshida describes have been evident in the United States since the turbulent 1960s and the Watergate scandal of the 1970s.

But there were two major differences. First, the rise of political independence in the United States reflected a partial realignment of political loyalties. Many independents were in fact in transit from one party to the other. This was especially true in the American South where conservative voters who had once expressed their preferences through the Democratic Party moved toward an increasingly conservative Republican Party. Independent status was frequently a way station between one party and the other.

Moreover, the increasingly ideological character of the two American parties actually deepened loyalties in certain respects. Since the 1950s, America has been a nation of ticket splitters in which many voters went one way in presidential elections and another in elections for Congress and state and local office. Since the end of the Reagan era, that tendency has begun to reverse and voters are casting more straight party tickets, especially in federal elections.

And however much party loyalties weakened, American voters—in Japanese terms, the "wind" voters—were, for the most part, willing to shift from one party to another when they felt a need to punish the incumbent government. Thus were the Republican Nixon-Ford years followed by the Democratic Carter years, which in turn were followed by the Republican Reagan-Bush years, the Democratic Clinton years, and now a new Republican presidency under a new Bush.

Still, if Japan has lacked a clear alternating party system, the rise of the Democratic Party of Japan (DPJ) might be seen as an important development—whether or not the party itself survives over the longer term. The very creation of a catch-all alternative party built pressure on the ruling elites. A wide range of voters used the DPJ to express their frustrations with the LDP. It is possible to argue that without the rise of the DPJ, Koizumi would have been impossible, even if Koizumi's success may now undermine the DPJ. The vote for the DPJ, along with protest votes cast earlier for other parties such as the New Frontier Party, sent a signal to the LDP leadership that there was a hunger for change. Koizumi, himself a shrewd reader of the public mood, no doubt received this signal, too. It is ironic—and a sign of the LDP's extraordinary ability to adjust to whatever circumstances come its way—that Koizumi's candidacy transformed the very party against which voters were protesting. "Koizumi's popularity stems from the anti-LDP sentiment," Yoshida writes. The LDP is the rare political party that won an election by running against itself.

In certain respects, of course, anti-party developments in Japan exactly match developments in virtually all other democracies, and these are rooted in general social changes rather than particular economic circumstances. When Yoshida describes the rise of television tabloid shows and when he speaks of tele-politics as speeding up the circulation of political news, he could be writing about the United States, France, the United Kingdom, or countless other nations where the mass media have, to some degree at least, displaced traditional party organizations. Such media can expose political shortcomings and corruption to a wide audience. It can also, at times, deepen political cynicism. Both are more devastating to political systems in times of economic crisis.

The volatility Yoshida sees in Japan is matched by a comparable volatility in many other democracies. And the sense that politics has become more unprincipled is fed by the decline of ideological politics and the consequent fraying of strong party loyalties. The paradox is that voters in many nations tell pollsters simultaneously that they miss a principled politics that they see as rooted in the ideological conflicts of the past, even as they also insist that they mistrust ideology. In Japan, the conflict was between an ideological politics on the left and the LDP's conservative pragmatism that involved using the state energetically on behalf of social order, economic growth, and established interests. Conservative pragmatism won for decades because it delivered the Japanese economic miracle.

When the miracle stopped, the left was no longer the major alternative in Japanese politics, but neither had it disappeared from the scene. Here again, one can see an important difference with the other democracies. In most of the West, the political left became steadily more moderate, adopting a third-way politics pioneered by Bill Clinton in the United States and Tony Blair in Britain. It entailed, in principle at least, an embrace of the market along with moderate government regulation and a modernized welfare state. This positioned the moderate left between an older left that favored greater government intervention in the economy and a new conservatism created by Ronald Reagan and Margaret Thatcher that supported a sharp reduction in the state's role. In Italy, the Italian Communist Party followed this model. It changed its name, heavily watering down its Marxism, and put itself at the heart of a new center-left bloc that eventually took power. That transformation called forth a reorganization on the center-right and the creation of a new electoral system.

But while the DPJ sometimes spoke of itself as a third-way party, the third way had only limited application to the Japanese circumstance. For it was the conservative party that had built an elaborate system of state intervention in the economy. When the economic miracle stopped, many in Japan and elsewhere placed the blame on a system of heavy state intervention on behalf of particular industries and an export-oriented economy. The third way's answers were a response to the different questions posed by a very different state-versus-market argument that dominated politics in most of the Western democracies.

Yet at a moment when many Japanese were already feeling overburdened, calls for deregulation promised not relief, but, as Yoshida writes, "greater burden and pain." It was thus logical, if somewhat surprising, that the LDP, the party of conservative pragmatism, transformed itself into the party of conservative populism. Stylistically, Koizumi appealed to a younger Japan that had grown impatient with gray personalities. Politically, he promised a revolution against the bureaucracy. But it was a revolution led by the party that had constructed the very system he pledged to uproot.

One can thus only agree with Yoshida that the nature of Koizumi's appeal and the fragility of the electoral constituency he built mean that many voters would be prepared, using his word, to "ditch" the LDP if they became dissatisfied with the results of his government. And here we return to where we started. It is highly unlikely that the old LDP system would have collapsed had economic growth continued. As Yoshida notes, "the Japanese postwar political process has been concerned with determining how to share the fruits of economic growth. Such a process was well met by the old way of politics, but those fruits began to shrivel about the time Japanese society began to turn gray."

Koizumi clearly has exceptional political skills. But the breakdown of the old system was caused precisely by its failure to create the fruits of economic growth that could be widely shared. Koizumi's primary task is to restore a period of growth. If he fails to do this reasonably quickly, the political wind that blew so many politicians in and out of the center of the country's political life will begin blowing again. It will then take all of Koizumi's talents for him to avoid being blown away as were so many of his predecessors.

4

Breaking the State Monopoly on Public Affairs

Katō Hideki

T H E 1990s have been called a "lost decade" for Japan. Certainly it was a period in which the country seemed to flounder without a clear, long-term strategic vision, scrambling to cope with the long recession that followed the burst of the bubble economy and with the various problems that then came percolating to the surface. In the political sphere, there was a succession of party realignments, changes of government, and reforms of the administrative setup, but none of them amounted to the real reform that people had hoped for.

The current decade may be seen as just the next act in the longer drama of Japan's post–World War II history. Half a century since the war's end, the cheery—and sometimes euphoric—first act ended. The second act has begun on a gloomy note. A whole series of "reforms" have been undertaken on an emergency or ad hoc basis to deal with the changing conditions of the moment. The January 2001 overhaul of the ministries and agencies of the central government, however, has been seen by many as yet another supposed reform that lacks real substance. And the National Public Service Ethics Law, adopted after scandals sullied the reputation of the bureaucracy, is viewed with even greater skepticism.

The background to each of these reform efforts, and the cool reception they have received, is similar. The media makes a great commotion over a problem without digging beneath the surface to uncover the deeper story. The ruling parties, which lack a solid base for their position in power, and the opposition parties, which lack a sense of direction, are swayed by the media uproar and cobble together a compromise set of measures designed more for show than for content. Meanwhile, the bureaucracy does its best to maintain the status quo. This—if I may offer my own media-style sketch—seems to be the common pattern. One wonders if the administrative setup will in fact be improved through this kind of repeated patching. But one can also take the view that there is no need to be so pessimistic. A picture can look quite different depending on the angle from which it is viewed.

Leaving aside the individual measures that have been taken and the results that they have produced or failed to produce up to now, if we turn our gaze to the broader current, we can see a certain coherence and inevitability in what is going on. What is happening is the emergence, in various forms, of the unsustainability of the approach that Japan has taken since the mid-nineteenth century in the name of modernization, that is, to have the government take charge of all public affairs. The fact that we are near the end of this particular road is something that not just politicians and bureaucrats but society as a whole must deal with. This broader view suggests that even though the individual measures implemented in the name of reform may in many respects be wasteful, ineffective, or even harmful, the overall current is moving in the direction it must. Looking at the reform process as a whole issue, we find that the second act of the drama is crucial in bringing Japan's modernization to a conclusion and switching to a greatly different set of economic, social, and political systems. Given the nature of this period and the fact that democracy is essentially a wasteful system, a certain amount of confusion and waste is only to be expected as part of the effort to achieve change. So, one wonders, is it appropriate for journalists and commentators to detachedly discuss those lost years?

THE STATE MONOPOLY ON PUBLIC AFFAIRS

Both Japanese and non-Japanese often remark that Japan is a country where people rely on the government, or *okami* (those on high), for everything. It is true that the government, national and local, is involved in a vast range of activities, from care for children and the elderly to implementation of public works projects, both directly and through the payment of subsidies. This is a state of affairs which most Japanese have grown accustomed to. Even the media, which trumpet small government, are quick to demand that authorities take responsibility when something goes wrong. And when the economy stalls, the government is expected to provide stimulus to promote a recovery. So pervasive is the hand of government that Japan has been called "the world's most successful socialist country."

Japan had a much smaller government in the Edo period (1600–1868), when the shogun and his vassals ruled as real *okami*. Regardless of the ostensible power of these overlords, the country's civil society had, in practice, a considerably broader reach than is the case today. All kinds of activities, ranging from the education of children and care for the infirm to local public works, were carried out in principle as "civilian" undertakings.

So how did the government end up getting its hand in everything? In recent years, talk of civil society has become all the rage, and nonprofit organizations (NPOs) have emerged as active players in various fields. Moves to regularize the status of NPOs are also progressing apace. This trend would seem to suggest the type of society Japan is headed toward. To understand this better, let us review the course Japan has followed since the Meiji era (1868–1912), when it embarked on its program of modernization.

Before the rise of the modern nation-state, the role of the national government was very limited, involving only internal security, diplomacy, and defense. Japan was a "night-watchman state." Under this setup, people basically took care of the public affairs affecting their own lives. Local communities, for the most part, handled disaster prevention and relief, public works, education, sanitation, town development, and assistance for the disabled and elderly. In the age of the night-watchman state, control of ordinary public affairs was highly decentralized, and the main actors were civil communities. This was true of traditional Japanese society as well.

Today, everyone thinks of the police, firefighters, schools, and public works as being naturally part of the government's domain. But in the Edo period, the bulk of these activities were in civilian hands. This is clear from the old terms used for the above four services: *meakashi* (police), *hikeshi* (firefighters), *terakoya* (schools), *jifushin* (public works).

All evoke the notion of community members working for the public interest, neither paid for nor controlled by the government. Of course there was no nationwide system of uniform public education, but in the mid-nineteenth century, some 70 percent to 80 percent of the children in Edo (present-day Tokyo) went to school, apparently a much higher rate than in Europe at the time. Textbooks on all kinds of subjects were prepared for the pupils of the *terakoya*; there are over seven thousand examples extant, and about a thousand were geared specifically for the education of girls.

To fight the fires for which Edo was famous, neighborhood residents throughout the city supported their own bands of *hikeshi*. While the two offices of magistrates administering Edo for the shogun were staffed by only a few hundred samurai in total, the city is said to have had almost ten thousand firefighters. The point is that both the *terakoya* teachers and the *hikeshi* were basically neighborhood volunteers whose reward was the respect and admiration of their community (see Ishikawa and Tanaka 1996).

Edo Japan was an absolute monarchy, where *okami* (the shogun and his retainers and vassals) controlled everything. Based on this fact, most Japanese believe they are a nation with a long tradition of relying on authorities to look after them. But closer examination of history reveals this to be incorrect. The role of *okami* was no more than the superficial control, under which the vast majority of public affairs was handled with complete autonomy by local communities. In addition to the four terms mentioned above, the vocabulary of the period included words like *yui*, *shū*, *kō*, and *kumi*, all referring to groups organized locally for joint undertakings of one kind or another. In other words, the basic setup was that ordinary citizens took care of virtually all public affairs relating to their lives.

Behind the transformation of this system of small government into the big government of the twentieth-century state lay the social changes that followed the industrial revolution. These included the rise of a population of factory workers and the progress of urbanization, accompanied by a widening income gap, the decline of traditional communities, and the emergence of problems like poor sanitation and crime in cities. At the same time, on the basis of their industrial power, countries competed intensively in the economic arena. In order to succeed, they needed proper roads, ports, and other infrastructure.

Meanwhile, in order to deal with rapid urbanization, assure workers a minimum standard of living, and build up national order, states found that they needed to provide various public services previously handled at the community level. This process, which led ultimately to the creation of the welfare state, meant the transfer of responsibility for public affairs from civilian to government hands. From the perspective of community residents, this represented the outsourcing of public activities previously handled by themselves.

In Japan's case, this process occurred in dramatic fashion, starting in the Meiji era as the country raced to catch up with the West. Because of the huge setback of World War II, it had to repeat much of the process after the war. During this period, the government adopted a variety of measures: an ever-growing volume of public works; industrial policy, starting with the priority production system that concentrated scarce resources for the development of core industries; the income-doubling plan of the 1960s and other economic policy; uniform nationwide education, in part to produce the workers required by industry; and the concentration of authority in the central government's hands to ensure that these policies would be implemented throughout the country. The strategy proved extremely effective—the economy grew very rapidly— but at the same time it sped up the further outsourcing of public affairs from the civil sector to the government. As this happened, the role communities had once played came to be rejected as premodern.

The result of this process then was a setup whereby the government monopolized the decisions as to what constituted the public interest as well as the actions carried out to serve this interest. Hoshino Eiichi (1998) refers to this as the "state monopoly on public affairs."

Japan has many arrangements institutionalizing this monopoly. Here are two critical examples: the provisions of Article 34 of the Civil Code and the establishment laws of the central government organs.

Article 34 of the Civil Code, which requires the approval of the competent authorities for the establishment of a public-interest corporation, has not been changed since it was promulgated in 1898. The article, in the archaic language of prewar legislation, declares: "Associations or foundations relating to ritual, religion, charity, academics, arts and crafts, or other fields of public interest and not having the purpose of seeking profits may be incorporated subject to the approval of the competent authorities." On the surface, the clause allows for the incorporation of public-interest organizations, but the deeper implication is that government determines the public interest. To administer this interest, the government creates uniform nationwide standards, and groups seeking to meet these standards apply for official approval.

The establishment laws of the central government organs define the roles and organization of ministries and agencies. This set of laws involves the core of Japan's system of governance, not just since the end of World War II but since the latter part of the nineteenth century. Two key terms in this regard are discretionary authority and administrative guidance, the latter being carried out on the basis of the former, which is broadly defined. Through administrative guidance, the organs of the central government exercise authority in ways that have not been specified under legislative provisions.

This authority has two sources. The first is the general provisions of individual laws, which grant authority to bureaucratic organs. The second is the establishment laws of each of the ministries and agencies that remained in effect until the revised laws in January 2001. In practice, most cases of administrative guidance have their basis in specific legislation, but the critical thing about establishment laws is that they gave bureaucrats sweeping, abstract powers that ranged across the entire scope of specific legislation.

How did these establishment laws work? Their fundamental purpose was to set the administrative responsibilities of each ministry or agency; in other words, they defined turf. They did not stop there, however; they also defined each organ's authority. For example, Article 4 of the original Ministry of Finance Establishment Law defines the ministry's functions to include "matters concerning the formulation of the national budget and settlement of accounts" and "matters concerning the imposition and collection of domestic taxes." Article 5 defined its corresponding powers to include the "formation of the national budget and settlement of accounts" and the "imposition and collection of domestic taxes."

Article 5 is the problem. Powers of the kind granted by Article 5 should, properly speaking, be based on specific fiscal and tax legislation. In a country under the rule of law, the powers of government organs are reasonably delimited by legal provisions, but the establishment laws for Japan's central government organs gives them comprehensive authority over the areas of their responsibility. They permit the sweeping exercise of administrative guidance.

There are many examples of administrative guidance given by ministries or agencies on the basis of establishment laws, but one of the better known is the system of acreage-reduction quotas for rice cultivation. Until the new Staple Food Law came into effect in 1995, there was no law specifically providing for reductions in the area of rice cultivation, but this did not stop the Ministry of Agriculture, Forestry and Fisheries from stipulating quotas. Another example involves nursing homes for the elderly. Medical corporations seeking to open such facilities have been subject to demands by the Ministry of Health and Welfare that the wishes of local physicians' groups be met; the Health and Medical Service Law for the Elderly contains no such provision.

Before police officials can search any premises in the investigation of a crime, a specific search warrant must be secured. If criminal investigators had the power to barge into a home or office without a search warrant, we would not be living in a country under the rule of law. Though this analogy may not be precise, the establishment laws of Japan's central government organs in effect gave bureaucrats that power.

While it may now be accepted that government organs must have the authority of specific legislation in order to act even within their areas of responsibility, from the Meiji era to the end of World War II, bureaucrats exercised governing authority and administrative powers as "officials of the emperor." Provisions establishing the bureaucracy were introduced at the time of the first Meiji government cabinet in 1885. These provisions, which defined the organization and powers of the bureaucracy, actually predate the creation of laws governing public administration, which occurred with the inauguration of the nation's first parliament in 1890.

Given its long tradition, that this system carried over into the postwar period as a part of Japan's distinctive set of generally accepted arrangements is not surprising. The problem is that public administration even today is performed as a natural extension of this archaic structure. Thus, until its revision in 2001, the Science and Technology Agency Establishment Law included a provision granting this agency power "to promote the use of space (except for matters under the responsibility of other administrative organs)." If this were taken at face value, the Japanese bureaucracy had the right to parcel out control not just of Japan but of the entire universe!

The bureaucratic setup in Japan accordingly has placed every aspect of national life under the purview of a government organ. Citizens and businesses depend on the government and are in turn controlled by it. The authority that bureaucrats have assumed affords them sweeping discretionary power, but it has also been reason for frequent cases of corruption. It also explains why deregulation and decentralization have failed to progress. For example, if the bureaucrats of the Ministry of Land, Infrastructure and Transport can dispense administrative guidance without any direct basis in the Road Transportation Law, then revising this law changes nothing.

It is true, of course, that everyday government administration is not conducted solely on the basis of the establishment laws. But these laws have been rather like water and air for the bureaucrats, and to a large degree, these laws sustain the bureaucrats still. The mandarins of the Ministry of Economy, Trade and Industry, for example, feel that anything relating to industrial policy or international trade is naturally their concern and their responsibility; the bureaucrats of the Ministry of Education, Culture, Sports, Science and Technology feel the same way about all matters relating to the school system. And on and on.

Both Article 34 of the Civil Code and the establishment laws of the central government organs served as the original institutional framework for the state monopoly on public affairs. This framework has since been filled out by a variety of other arrangements, such as central government subsidies and revenue sharing for local governments. By providing subsidies, the central government determines the shape of public services provided locally, leaving no room for regional discretion. The revenue sharing that is carried out under the local allocation tax theoretically provides funds for local authorities to use as they see fit. But here, too, the bulk of the money goes for the provision of services mandated by the central government, and the apportionment of the revenues is based on uniform standards for services in line with the goal of equal development throughout the country. Here again is a demonstration of the central government claiming the right and duty to decide the public interest.

From Outsourcing to "Insourcing"

Even as Japanese have relied on the government to handle tasks that properly should be carried out by the general public or by local communities, this policy was an efficient and fair approach in promoting national development. But during the long period that this setup has been operative, great changes have taken place in people's values and in national and global conditions; meanwhile, the organizational units and functions of the bureaucracy have proliferated, and the interests served have become ossified. As a result, the system of public administration has become overgrown, inefficient, and inequitable, and it has been sapping the vitality of the nation. This has led to drives for privatization, small government, and decentralization.

The reliance on the government to handle public affairs has also led to the hollowing out of community and individual life. The transformation from the Edo-style community groups that fulfilled community functions to the present system of outsourcing, where things are left to the government, was considered part of the process of modernization. But as a result of this process, communication among residents of local communities was attenuated.

After the Kobe earthquake in January 1995, rescue efforts reportedly went more smoothly in the older districts of the city, where people knew their neighbors. While modern Japanese seem to prefer an anonymous, independent lifestyle to the community of the old-fashioned village, where nothing can be kept secret, this trend has not been without cost. Leaving aside the issue of disaster relief (knowing whom to search for where in a jumble of collapsed buildings), we encounter various problems born of this mutual alienation, including something as mundane as getting people to sort their trash properly before putting it out for collection. We also see disregard for social rules, bad etiquette, and ill manners.

Without harking back to the Edo period, surely many people have enjoyed a small but warm feeling of satisfaction from giving and receiving bits of help in neighborhood relationships. Opportunities for interchanges of this kind, however, are few. The recent popularity of involvement in NPOs may be, at least in part, a result of an attempt to fill the void left by the social atomization of modern life.

What can we do to counter this situation and develop a civil society in today's Japan? A variety of moves are already under way, including activities by NPOs and nongovernmental organizations (NGOs) on both the domestic and international fronts. Overall, the process we need to encourage is one that switches back to the "insourcing" of everyday, local activities. To put it in political terms, we must seek a transformation away from a society where the state holds a monopoly on public affairs to one where public affairs are decided and implemented by the people whose interests are at stake.

As discussed above, the provisions of the establishment laws vesting general powers in ministries and agencies were abolished in 2001. This was the result of the efforts of the group Japan Initiative, which I am a member of. The ideal approach to reform would be to eliminate these laws altogether, but with the abolition of the general-powers provisions, all that remains is the assignment of functional responsibility to particular organs. Unlike quantitative change, such as reducing the number of concerns subject to bureaucratic approval or narrowing the scope of administrative guidance, this change represents a revolution in the relationship between the government and the people. It should transform the mind-set of bureaucrats, who will no longer hold the scepter of authority, as well as the attitude of the general public.

The effect of this change may not be seen immediately. But the culture of dependence and control that has prevailed since the latter part of the nineteenth century is about to lose its structural backbone. I am confident that this reform will be of tremendous significance in the history of Japan's system of governance.

While incremental changes are required—such as the system by which the central government sets the level of costs for local services—various institutional changes are necessary as well. The revision of Article 34 of the Civil Code, which goes a long way toward reconceiving the role of the state in public affairs, is at a critical juncture. Known as the NPO Law, the Law to Promote Specified Nonprofit Activities went into effect in December 1998. The review of the law's supplementary resolution concerning tax provisions resulted in the 2001 Law Amending in Part the Special Tax Measures Law. This law took effect from October, but the requirements to qualify for tax breaks are so strict that most NPOs do not qualify.

Some background should clarify the situation. Corporations fall into two broad categories: for-profit and nonprofit. For-profits are ordinary business enterprises as specified under the Commercial Code, and incorporation can be done simply by registration. Nonprofits, however, could be incorporated only if approved as a public-interest corporation under Article 34 of the Civil Code or under special legislation. The NPO Law has changed this situation somewhat, the requirement for official approval replaced with a requirement for "authentication," which is a less rigorous procedure. Today, a body may become incorporated even without the recognition of the government that its activities serve the public interest.

Public-interest corporations created under the earlier law are eligible for tax breaks and other favorable treatment. They are also subject to almost no monitoring as to whether their activities continue to serve the public interest. Essentially, the incorporation process and the certification of public-interest activities were the same procedure. Corporations set up under the NPO Law and unincorporated nonprofit groups, on the other hand, receive no tax breaks, even if their activities are in fact in the public interest.

To rectify this inequity, Japan Initiative has recommended that Article 34 of the Civil Code be revised so that the incorporation process for nonprofit corporations follows that of for-profit corporations. Accordingly, the provision of tax breaks and other favorable treatment would then be based on whether the body's activities were truly in the public interest.

Who would make this determination, and on what basis? The public interest is not an abstract, indeterminate whole. Any single set of standards adopted to judge the full range of activities across the country is therefore bound to run into spots where the standards do not apply. What is needed instead is a set of rules and procedures that actively involve members of the public whose interests are the real issue.

To this end, Japan Initiative has proposed the creation of independent public-interest accreditation committees in each of the forty-seven prefectures. These committees would determine the qualification of NPO activities, and government organs would provide tax breaks and the like on the basis of what these committees decide. The city of Abiko, Chiba Prefecture, has in fact passed a municipal ordinance that puts much of this proposal into practice, starting in fiscal 2000. The mayor has appointed a five-member committee, consisting of academic experts and people with experience in public administration, whose charge will be to assess publicly solicited applications for municipal subsidies. Subsidies will be granted based on the committee's decisions.

Inasmuch as the members are appointed by the mayor, the committee may not be independent in the strict sense of the term. Further, how they are chosen, what their qualifications are, and what procedures the committee operates under—all must be subject to open accountability. Despite the need for fine-tuning, however, the Abiko model goes a long way toward involving the public in the determination of the public interest.

A JAPANESE REVIVAL

In the United States, local governments often form panels of citizens to take part in the decision-making process. In Japan as well, the voices of citizens are now being heard in the example of Abiko. If independent committees like this were formed at the national level, then we could say that Japan will have broken away from the state monopoly on public affairs.

To sum up, the core of civil society lies in a set of arrangements that provide autonomy for local communities. In the past, the neighborhoods in cities and towns and hamlets were Japan's communities. Now, however, there is not even a proper Japanese word for "community"; the English word instead is used to express the concept. At least for the past half century, Japanese have lived without thinking about activities that should be conducted through joint social efforts or about collective units that should serve as the vehicle for such efforts. But it is only through joint activities in communities that Japan can hope to rebuild its social conventions. The fact that many people are now participating in NPOs and other forms of volunteer activity seems to represent a desire for the satisfaction that comes from joint endeavors. As I see it, however, in order to achieve a true "Japanese revival," the society must be one where such community activities become a normal part of everyday life.

Put another way, the nation must adopt a clearer vision of the balance between what citizens need to do for local society and what citizens can expect that society to do for them. Instead of having to choose between a "high welfare, high burden" society and a "low welfare, low burden" one, the nation might think to create a "low cost, high satisfaction" society. Citizens would enjoy a high level of autonomy, free from dependence on or control by the government, and at the same time they would have much closer ties with each other.

Obviously my points are not just a set of arguments about systems of the state. The issues I have raised concern the setup of Japanese society that needs to be addressed through individual activities in everyday lives. Without proper social systems, the foundation of the nation will collapse. And inasmuch as the prosperity of the nation depends on the creation and maintenance of such social systems, the biggest issue for Japanese politics at the start of the twenty-first century should be to determine how the national and local governments can contribute to this cause.

BIBLIOGRAPHY

Hoshino Eiichi. 1998. *Minpō no susume* (A recommendation of the Civil Code). Tokyo: Iwanami Shoten.

Ishikawa Eisuke and Tanaka Yukō. 1996. *O-Edo borantia jijō* (Edo volunteerism). Tokyo: Kodansha.

Japan Initiative's Legislative Council. 1997. Minkan hōsei shingikai hōkokusho: Kōkatsudo no kiban seibi ni kansuru hōritsu an (Report of Japan Initiative's Legislative Council: A proposal concerning infrastructure for activities in the public interest). Tokyo: Japan Initiative.

5

The Tides of Reform Arrive in Japan

Paul C. Light

LIKE the United States, Japan is currently being buffeted by enormous pressure for change. Economic and social distress has increased the public demand for reforms of any kind, and the Japanese state has responded with a reform for any philosophy. As Katō Hideki writes, "A whole series of 'reforms' have been undertaken on an emergency or ad hoc basis to deal with changing conditions of the moment."

Katō's description of the reforms is eerily familiar to my own research on the tides of administrative reform in the United States at all levels of government. As I wrote in 1997, the problem at the national level of government is not too little reform, but too much: "Congress and the presidency have had little trouble passing reform measures over the years, moving almost effortlessly from one reform philosophy to another and back again, rarely questioning the contradictions and consequences of each separate act. If government is not getting better, it is most certainly not for a lack of legislation."*

The same might be said of Japan, which appears to be catching up to the United States in the sheer velocity of reform. The four "tides" of

*Light, Paul C. 1997. *The Tides of Reform: Making Government Work, 1945–1995*. New Haven, Conn.: Yale University Press. p. 1.

administrative reform, as delineated below, have all made their way to Japan in recent years, most likely from the global network of organizational theorists who have yet to reach any agreement on what kinds of reforms might improve government performance under which circumstances.

TIDES OF TRUST

The first tide, which I have labeled "scientific management," shows up early in Katō's chapter in a reference to the January 2001 reorganization of the central government, which Katō argues is now seen by many observers "as yet another supposed reform that lacks real substance." This tide is based on the notion that administrative performance is to be found in the proper—that is, scientific—reorganization of government bureaus into a more centralized, accountable organization chart.

The well-worn history of scientific management in the United States has been viewed with similar disdain. Congress and the president have organized and reorganized the boxes of the organization chart with stunning frequency, putting like units together into mega-departments that offer the promise of close coordination, clear chains of command, and undisputed leadership from the top. That was certainly the promise of the reorganization of the U.S. national government in response to the two national commissions chaired by former President Herbert Hoover in the 1950s.

All told, under the presidencies of Harry Truman, Dwight Eisenhower, and John Kennedy, there were thirty-nine reorganization plans implemented during 1949–1961, even as Congress passed a dozen separate laws, building new departments and reorganizing old ones around a carefully crafted organization chart that promised concentrated authority and accountability. Every department was to have a secretary, supported by an undersecretary, and a small number of assistant secretaries that would allow the president to reach every last person in the organization through order. The product was a cleaner organizational chart composed of new departments such as Defense and Health, Education, and Welfare, and streamlined versions of old departments such as Commerce, State, and Treasury.

It was not long, however, before Congress and the president concluded that decentralization and devolution was the answer. Just as Japan is now considering what Katō describes as "insourcing," the United States soon decided that the organization chart was too tight and shifted attention to devolving responsibilities to state and local government and splitting departments. This effort to relax control through what I have labeled "liberation management" can be seen in a host of initiatives, whether in Richard Nixon's "new federalism" program, which endeavored to collapse giant categorical, or strings-attached, grant programs to state and local government into highly flexible block grants, or in Vice President Al Gore's reinventing-government campaign, which promised to give federal managers the freedom to manage.

Scientific management and liberation management clearly operated under very different philosophies of reform. Whereas scientific management sought to impose standard procedures on all departments, whether in the form of a single organization chart or precise rules for all forms of administrative behavior, liberation management sought to free agencies from the strait jacket imposed by central management control. What scientific management put together to eliminate duplication and impose scientific theory on personnel, financial management, procurement, and a host of other administrative functions, liberation management sought to divide through decentralization and weakening of central management agencies such as the U.S. Office of Management and Budget and the Office of Personnel Management.

Scientific management and liberation management do have one characteristic in common, however. They both trust the government to perform with minimal external review. They view government employees as basically well motivated by the public good, and their executives as competent to supervise governmental activities with minimal outside review.

TIDES OF DISTRUST

Even as scientific management and liberation management have ebbed and flowed through the U.S. government, two tides have made their mark on the administrative infrastructure. Unlike the other tides, these find their strength in a general distrust of government and its employees to do the right thing.

One is what I call "watchful eye," which is based on the theory that administrative performance is enhanced by introducing greater sunshine in government. This appears to be the central thrust of Japan's recent National Public Service Ethics Law. Like the U.S. Ethics in Government Act of 1978, this recent Japanese reform puts its faith in public disclosure (sunshine) as an instrument of increased accountability. Only by making the invisible visible can citizens and the media have confidence that government is behaving well, and only by injecting what one U.S. official described as the "visible odium of deterrence" can administrative officers be frightened into good behavior.

Ethics in government is only one part of the watchful-eye philosophy. Freedom of information, increased audit and investigation activity, and greater competition for contracts and grants are all seen as essential to improved performance. So, too, is a complex system of notification and review for making rules under the Administrative Procedure Act.

The other tide of distrust is known as "war on waste," reflecting the persistent belief in the United States that government is incapable of spending money wisely. It is best represented by the repeated hiring and pay freezes that have pulsed through the U.S. government since the post–World War II demobilization. War on waste is based on the political economy of bureaucracy—that is, the simple premise that government executives and workers are motivated by an unyielding desire for self-aggrandizement and power that can only be tempered by constant vigilance and downsizing.

WHEN THE TIDES COLLIDE

There are four problems associated with the tides of reform in the United States that offer warning to Japan as the pressure for reform accelerates. First, the tides of reform often operate independently of each other. There are constituents for each of the tides, which produce nearly unending competition among each of the reform philosophies over time. Because the United States rarely repeals past reforms before enacting new reforms, the result is a steady accretion of reform over time. The result has been a thickening of the federal hierarchy with endless statutory requirements to serve each of the four tides, which, in turn, prompts frequent effort to fix the problems that arise from the competition.

Second, administrative reform in the United States and Japan is rarely tried on a limited, experimental basis before being adopted government-wide. Reform is almost always implemented for every agency at the same time, which increases the burden of actually administering the reform. The political rationale is simple: if ethics reform is good for one department or ministry, it must be good for all; if reorganization is good for a handful of agencies, it should yield even greater results for all.

Third, it should be obvious by now that the four tides of reform offer contradictory messages to government on how to increase performance. Scientific management instructs presidents to centralize, while liberation management encourages decentralization; watchful eye promotes visibility and sunshine, while war on waste focuses on reducing staff and eliminating needless oversight. Although the four tides can coexist, the contradictions often undermine the potential for any one reform to generate enough momentum to succeed.

Finally, as Katō notes, the pressure to reform appears to be accelerating over time, meaning that the amount of time between the last reform agenda and the next is decreasing. The result is a constant flood of reform that confuses agencies, distorts priorities, and leaves little room for determining whether a given reform actually works.

A CAUTIONARY NOTE

Japan appears to be at a moment when there might still be time to avert the problems associated with the tides of reform in the United States. Unlike the U.S. national government, which has been awash in competing tides for the better part of a half century, Japan is just starting to sort out the administrative reforms that it deems essential for higher bureaucratic performance. If there is one lesson in the confused history of reforms in the United States, it is to be cautious about both the number of reforms to be introduced at any one time and the contradictions between them. Reform needs at least some time to take hold. By introducing one reform after another, Japan could easily find itself facing the same problem that now plagues U.S. administrative life: not too little reform, but too much.

6

Changes in the Japanese Policymaking Process

Shiozaki Yasuhisa

F OR Japan, the last ten years of the twentieth century are now referred to as the "lost decade." All of us are familiar with the economic dimensions of the lost decade: namely, a lackluster economy, deflation, bankruptcies, rising unemployment, and a fragile banking system. But the decade was lost in political terms as well. During this period, there were seven prime ministers before the current incumbent, Koizumi Jun'ichirō. Their average duration in office was 495 days—too brief for a prime minister to deliver his own policy program, if not someone else's. Policy swung and swayed—from Hashimoto Ryūtarō's tightening of fiscal policy to Obuchi Keizō's loosening of fiscal policy, and now back to tightening again under the Koizumi administration.

Koizumi became prime minister in April 2001 on a platform of reform. This has helped him gain tremendous popularity among average Japanese, even as the specifics of his reform plan have yet to be put into practice.

I am committed to fully supporting Prime Minister Koizumi's reform, but I am not entirely sure about its rapid implementation. For one thing, Koizumi's plan is so ambitious and sweeping that it will affect much of the bureaucracy as well as many interest groups hostile to any major change in the status quo. The history of Japanese politics tells us that an administration can usually accomplish only one large task and therefore a leader must prioritize. The Koizumi administration has put more emphasis on fiscal consolidation than on resolution of the non-performing loan problem. It is my view that the latter is, by far, the policy issue of greatest priority, essential for enhancing productivity and profitability. Further, any implementation of structural reform warrants full attention to the dynamics of the global economy as well.

CHARACTERISTICS OF THE LOST DECADE

THE END OF THE "IRON TRIANGLE"

Another source of uncertainty over the prospect of reform lies in the fundamental decision-making process in Japan's politics. Except for some highly sensitive issues, such as constitutional amendments and the introduction of the consumption tax, the government has been known—until 1993 when the Liberal Democratic Party (LDP) lost its majority—for making decisions and implementing policies with expedition.

Under the old regime, big businesses, bureaucrats, and politicians had a congenial relationship referred to as the "iron triangle." The groups shared two common objectives: anti-communism and catching up with the West economically. When opinion on issues differed, top politicians of the LDP and top business leaders would meet informally to make what would become final decisions. Top bureaucrats may have had influence, but the decision making itself was done by the political and business leaders. Once a decision was made, it was formalized by due democratic procedure, that is, through discussion and vote in the Diet. Since the LDP controlled the Diet by a comfortable majority, the outcome was certain.

In the 1980s, the two common objectives of the iron triangle were achieved: Japan caught up with the West economically, and the Berlin Wall was torn down. Although this joint focus was no longer, the iron triangle retained its power, which even increased temporarily. This was evident, for example, in the early months of the Hosokawa Morihiro administration when the Ministry of Finance and the policy caucus members of the Diet flexed considerable political muscle.

This situation did not last long, however. Two axioms held: First, that absolute power corrupts absolutely, and second, that fish rots from the head.

Soon after the power of the iron triangle peaked, it fell sharply in the face of a series of scandals. In 1989, the Recruit stocks-for-favors scandal brought down both the Ministry of Labor and the Ministry of Education. In 1995, the Ministry of Health and Welfare suffered in the shadow of the AIDS tainted-blood scandal. Even the highly respected Ministry of Finance and Bank of Japan were ravaged by scandal. In recent months, the Ministry of Foreign Affairs has been wallowing in scandal after scandal, as has the Postal Services Agency because of its illegal involvement in the House of Councillors election of 2001. In the course of events, politicians and high-ranking officials have been arrested or forced to step down.

This state of affairs may be the result of a lack of a control tower, or a beacon, in government. Under the iron triangle system, political leaders such as Takeshita Noboru and a few intellectual bureaucrats conducted government policy as if it were a national beacon, but this guiding principle is no longer. The death of guru politics may be viewed as democratic progress, but the present system is unhealthy. Now, less prominent political figures concentrate on their political survival by making alliances with ad hoc policymaking units.

THE AD HOC POLICYMAKING MACHINE

The series of scandals fueled public resentment of the iron triangle in general and the LDP in particular, which has made it difficult for the LDP to capture a majority in the House of Representatives since 1993. Policy under these circumstances has been decided on an ad hoc basis. Under the Hashimoto administration, for example, younger politicians and bureaucrats played an important role in policy decisions as well as policy planning. Under the Obuchi administration, coalition partners of the LDP played a significant role. Under the Mori Yoshirō administration, the Policy Research Council of the LDP, headed by Kamei Shizuka, was instrumental in policymaking.

In the first several months of the Koizumi administration, the Prime

Minister's Office seems to be most influential, but it is too early to know for certain. Many academics and private advisors work in the Prime Minister's Office, but no one can tell who, other than bureaucrats, really shapes an administration's central doctrine on matters such as the ¥30 trillion ceiling on the annual bond issuance. When key actors have changed in the last decade, decisions of the government have been made on an ad hoc basis, depending on the power structure of each administration.

DETERIORATION OF THE GOVERNMENT'S POLITICAL POWER BASE

Associated with the ad hoc feature of decision making is the fact that each government since the Hosokawa administration has ended up weakening its own power base. For example, in February 1994 the Hosokawa administration suddenly proposed an increase in the consumption tax under the name of the "national welfare tax." This grossly unpopular proposal, coupled with a series of internal conflicts among the coalition parties, brought down the non-LDP coalition, putting the LDP back in power four months later.

The next prime minister, Murayama Tomiichi, had been head of the then Social Democratic Party of Japan (SDPJ), which had long denounced the U.S.-Japan Security Treaty as well as the Self-Defense Forces (SDF). Murayama endorsed both the treaty and the SDF, thereby forgoing the socialist credo. As a result, the SDPJ lost so many seats in the following general election that it was reduced to a very small party.

Shortly after Hashimoto became prime minister in early 1996, he proposed an ambitious reform package, an unprecedented act for an LDP prime minister selected through due process. I took part in his financial reform, which was called the Big Bang, as well as in the revision of the Bank of Japan Law and the creation of the Financial Supervisory Agency. By trying for so ambitious a plan, however, Hashimoto cut off the well-established linkages between the bureaucracy and policy caucus members of the Diet, alienating both and contributing to his downfall.

Under the Obuchi and Mori administrations, government spending increased dramatically. In this period, the idiosyncrasies of the public works programs became apparent, leading to the review of public works under Koizumi.

All this is as ironic as it is paradoxical, but an important question arises now with respect to what Koizumi is going to destroy. There is the chance that the Koizumi administration will end up destroying the LDP's traditional power base: farmers, small shop owners, and small manufacturing and construction firms. Koizumi himself has suggested as much by saying, "Let us change the LDP, thus let us change Japan."

Ad hoc decision making and deteriorating power bases have characterized Japan's politics during the lost decade. Will a new decision-making process be established in the near future? What kind of policymaking process is emerging now as a model for the future of Japan?

New Features

The Diet used to be called a rubber stamp because the vast majority of government-sponsored bills were voted on and agreed to in the Diet without revision. However, under the ad hoc policymaking process in the past decade, the Diet has emerged with a new cast.

"brats in the diet"

The political process that in 1998 produced the Comprehensive Plan for Financial Revitalization (the so-called Total Plan) for resolution of nonperforming asset problems and the subsequent Financial Revitalization Law (FRL) marked the beginning of a new style of policymaking in Japan. Traditionally, in Japanese politics, only party leaders collaborated to maintain a status quo environment; the ruling party paved the way and opposition parties agreed reluctantly. However, on this particular occasion, a group of junior politicians with policy expertise—known as the *seisaku shinjinrui*, or "brats in the Diet"—were able to take action themselves, thus generating a new approach in policymaking among bureaucrats, the ruling party, and opposition parties.

These are the details: Within a week after the Obuchi cabinet was installed, the bill regarding emergency measures for the revitalization of the financial system (which was to become the FRL) was submitted to the Diet on August 5, 1998. The FRL, originally drafted by the Ministry of Finance, included the bridge bank scheme for the resolution of bad loans. By that time, however, the Long-Term Credit Bank of Japan (LTCB) was showing signs of failing and the Ministry of Finance tried to rescue it by injecting public capital and forcing a merger with the

Sumitomo Trust Bank. The plan did not succeed. The Ministry of Finance had wished to discuss the LTCB issue separately from the FRL legislation and, therefore, proposed only the bridge bank scheme, because, as a practical matter, the scheme was geared mainly to small banks, not to large money centers like the LTCB.

Junior politicians within the LDP had other ideas. They tacked on a nationalization scheme to the FRL legislation that could be applied to the LTCB. This was welcomed by both financial markets and public opinion, which were pleased for the departure from the ministry's policy of pampering the banks. In fact, these junior LDP politicians had developed the Total Plan approach to the nonperforming assets problem in the beginning of 1998. The plan included a strict due-diligence measure for nonperforming assets, the establishment of debt-servicing companies, and drastic improvements in bankruptcy proceedings, all of which were a change from the past policy of forbearance and were intended to push the ministry and banking industry toward a fundamental resolution of nonperforming loans. The important point here is that it was not only the opposition party members who took issue with the bureaucrats' plan; strong objections were also raised within the LDP.

All major parties agreed to the FRL on September 26, 1998. The most striking aspect of the outcome was the fact that the final bill was based on drafts from both the LDP and opposing parties. It included both bridge bank and nationalization schemes. The bureaucrats had to implement, almost unconditionally, a law devised by junior politicians from both the LDP and opposition parties. The LTCB was nationalized and its nonperforming assets fully removed under the application of the FRL. The case was unprecedented.

Several factors account for how these "brats in the Diet" came to play a major role in legislating the FRL. First, although they were inexperienced, their main asset actually was their expertise. Whereas senior politicians obtain their information mainly from bureaucrats, the younger generation of politicians approaches a wide spectrum of sources, both in and out of the country, to obtain the necessary knowledge and information.

Second, they were flexible. No matter their party affiliation, they worked to create a better FRL. Because they acted as public spokesmen, inter-party debate and negotiation became possible. Third, with their expertise and flexibility, these junior politicians developed a practical vision for fundamental policy change. Also it should be noted that the then party leaders, Katō Kōichi in the LDP and Kan Naoto in the Democratic Party of Japan (DPJ), allowed these junior politicians to play a significant role in the policy debate, perhaps because of the sense of urgency generated by the financial crisis in the global markets.

Some argue that the FRL would not have passed the Diet without the *seisaku shinjinrui*. After the FRL passed, senior politicians and factional politics regained power and junior politicians were removed from center stage of the policymaking process. Soon after Obuchi formed a coalition government with the New Kōmeitō and the Liberal Party, these "brats in the Diet" lost their influence on policymaking. Junior politicians possess expertise without power; senior politicians possess power without expertise. This is one of the most persistent and daunting dilemmas in Japanese politics.

POLITICAL APPOINTEES AND BUREAUCRATS

One of the characteristics of the policymaking process of the last decade is the involvement of an increasing number of non-bureaucrats. These non-bureaucrats, however, were not necessarily political appointees; in many cases bureaucrats, not politicians, appoint outsiders as a way to maintain their own influence. In any case, expert opinion is now more respected and required than in the past, partly as a consequence of increased transparency. When a wider audience keeps an eye on the substance of policy discussions, greater value is placed on expert opinion, irrespective of seniority in the old hierarchy.

On the other hand, bureaucratic apathy is increasingly more evident. Bureaucrats have recently been trying to hide behind the ad hoc decision-making machine, which consists of politicians, academics, and other non-bureaucrats, so as to minimize public criticism and personal accountability. Since bureaucrats live in the fragmented field of government functions, they tend to stay away from the areas of other ministries. This is one of the reasons why strong political leadership is needed. Fragmentation leads to delays or even stalemates in policy implementation because legislators make laws and cabinet members make policy decisions, but neither can be implemented without the bureaucracy. When the bureaucracy is apathetic or fragmented, policy is left unimplemented. Since structural reform requires a set of policy packages beyond the boundary of ministries, the forbearance that has been the usual attitude of bureaucrats works as an impediment.

POLITICAL REALIGNMENT

There have been several political party realignments since the big split in the LDP in 1993. Realignments among parties are likely to continue. However, such realignments may not be based on policy preferences, such as hawks versus doves on security issues, or liberals versus conservatives on economic policy. Party realignments are more likely to be based on personal relationships, and coalition governments will continue to be based more on political convenience than on policy.

Proposals

For a more accountable policymaking process in the Japanese government, politicians who are chosen by voters must play a more important role. The Diet must no longer be a mere rubber stamp of bureaucrat-made policy. Political reforms that permit and encourage politicians to work as genuine lawmakers are needed. Following are several proposals that might help.

INTEGRATION OF RULING PARTIES
AND THE GOVERNMENT

First, integrate the ruling parties and the government in order to strengthen the leadership of the prime minister. This cannot be achieved without decreasing the practice of the ruling party's pre-clearance of cabinet-sponsored bills before submission to the Diet. At the same time, efforts need to be made toward democratizing the Diet in order to facilitate productive debate and amendments under a more transparent system.

Currently, the ordinary Diet session is held only in the first half of the year, while the following year's budget process begins in the second half of the year. Under this system, the tax council in the ruling party discusses tax code changes only between October and December. Thus, LDP debates on budget appropriations and tax policy are held only in the fourth quarter, giving bureaucrats the freedom to operate without the constraints of political debate during the rest of the year. A year-round Diet can be a more accountable system, preventing the current tactical scheduling of the governing parties to pass as many pieces of legislation as possible within a limited time frame.

PRIME MINISTER'S OFFICE
AND MINISTERIAL STAFF

Second, strengthen the Prime Minister's Office. It is essential to restore the leadership of the office by increasing the number of expertise-based political appointees and non-bureaucrat advisors in the Prime Minister's Office, and possibly in individual ministries as well. The current system of deputy minister and parliamentary vice-minister may not function well because politicians can be easily deprived of access to timely, unbiased, and adequate information, let alone new ideas independent of the bureaucracy, needed to make their final decisions. On this point, minister and vice-ministers must form a team in directing bureaucrats. (Ministers are free to appoint whomever they wish as their assistant, but no minister has done so, probably because it means replacing civil servants.) Also, the introduction of an advisory committee with full-time membership, similar to the United Kingdom's Policy Unit, at the Prime Minister's Office deserves serious consideration.

STRENGTHEN THINK TANKS

Third, widen the policymaking community. Strengthening the intellectual base of national policymaking cannot be achieved without a strong and diverse think-tank community. Japanese think tanks tend to be affiliates of financial institutions or business associations. More independent, strategic think tanks should be cultivated as they would enhance the national debate.

DISCLOSURE

Lastly, disclosure has grown in importance in the Japanese political scene. As mentioned above, the last decade was mired in scandal, which fueled public mistrust of the iron triangle. The good thing, however, has been an increase in the transparency of public policymaking. In recent years, virtually all government councils and committees disclose the minutes of their meetings. Public comments are solicited with respect to policy drafts. Under these circumstances, individual policies can be decided on after due consideration of the issues and interests in question rather than by bargaining behind the scenes.

CONCLUSION

Japan's policymaking process is becoming more democratic in both good and bad senses. Until a new regime is established, the current chaotic situation will continue. Should we be happy about it, or at least accept it as it is? The answer is clearly no. In addition to being riddled by bureaucratic apathy and ad hoc processes, decision making is extremely messy and time consuming. Japan has no time to lose in putting its economy, national security, and society back on the right track, and under these circumstances someone has to lead—to help forge wise and timely policies and see to their effective implementation.

That someone is, of course, the prime minister. Fortunately, Japan has a tremendously popular prime minister at the moment. The time is right for gathering the best and the brightest from both inside and outside the government and marshalling their efforts for policy development and implementation. The main problem is not an inability to envision solutions, but an inability to put them into practice. Behind this inability lies weakness in our governance system involving politicians, bureaucrats, and constituencies. But pressure for change is intensifying among voters. It is of utmost importance today to institutionalize a new style of governance, one that can realize the grand vision of Japan embraced by the prime minister and one that revitalizes Japanese democracy.

7

The Promise and Peril of Legislative Reform

James M. Lindsay

J APAN'S policymaking process is in trouble, according to Shiozaki Yasuhisa, a Liberal Democratic Party (LDP) member of the
House of Representatives. The iron triangle of big business, bureaucrats, and politicians that dominated Japanese politics for decades relied
on a consensus about the need to catch up economically with the West
and to resist communist expansion. But Japan's economic prosperity
and the Soviet Union's collapse rendered these goals obsolete and, in
turn, robbed the iron triangle of the ideological glue that held it together.

With no new consensus developing, Japan now lacks a beacon or control tower in government. What has arisen instead is an ad hoc policymaking process. The dominant guru has been replaced by a multitude
of smaller gurus, each more interested in his political survival than in the
common good. The key players have changed with each shift in prime
minister. The *seisaku shinjinrui*, or "brats in the Diet"—a group of junior
politicians with policy expertise—have sought to carve out a greater
role for themselves but have found themselves outflanked by more senior politicians. Policy reforms have faltered, and Japan continues to
grapple with fundamental economic and political problems.

The situation Shiozaki describes sounds more familiar than strange
to an American ear. One does not have to try too hard to find echoes

of similar problems in the past operations of the U.S. Congress. This is not to say that American political practice provides a direct analogue. The differences between the American and Japanese political systems and cultures are too great for that to be the case. Yet there are enough similarities between the two that a review of how Congress dealt with a major shift two decades ago may contain valuable insights—and cautions—for Japan.

The Centralized Congress

The U.S. Congress today has a well-deserved reputation as a democratic institution. True, members of Congress are not all created equal, and seniority typically brings additional status and influence. But one of the most remarkable features of today's Congress is how quickly even the newest members of the House and Senate can become crucial policy players.

This has not always been how things operated on Capitol Hill, however. Until the 1970s, congressional decision making was relatively centralized. Committees dominated congressional business, and senior members, especially the chairs, dominated committee business. House and Senate rules gave chairs tremendous power. They could create and abolish subcommittees, set committee agendas, choose committee staff, and manage bills when they went to the floor. Informal norms of behavior reinforced these formal rules; junior committee members were expected to view their tenure as an apprenticeship and to defer to committee leaders.

Not surprisingly, many committee chairs ran their committees as personal baronies—their word was law. Most consulted only with other senior members, but not with junior members. In the case of the House Armed Services Committee, for instance, members had to serve for as long as ten years before they were allowed to play a major role in committee business. One junior member complained in 1969:

> But we have another thing on our committee. It is called the policy committee . . . I do not know what it is. I have been on the [Armed Services] committee only 4½ years. I do not know who the members of the policy committee are. . . . I have never seen a scratch of a pen before our committee authorizing what the policy

committee does. I know on the day of our committee markup [of the defense spending bill] it was reported to us that the policy committee had recommended such and such with respect to all of these various systems, but I have never heard one member of the policy committee ... relate what was happening, relate an argument, or relate some of the democracy that has taken place on that very important committee. (*Congressional Record* 1969)

Things were much the same in the Senate, which was characterized as an elite men's club in which a handful of senior members dominated decisions (see Matthews 1960; White 1956). One senator described his experience as a junior member of the Senate Committee on Armed Services in the 1960s as follows: "[Chairman Richard] Russell and the senior members would sit at the other end. I'm partially deaf in my right ear and I couldn't even hear what the hell was going on. Finally one day I spoke up and asked Russell if he would mind talking louder so we could hear what decisions were being made!" (Lindsay 1991, 29).

In addition to the considerable deference from junior committee members, senior committee members could often expect considerable deference from the parent chamber. Floor challenges to committee bills were more the exception than the rule. In many cases, the bill the committee wrote became the bill that the chamber passed. To some extent, this floor deference reflected agreement on the merits of the policy and on what committee chairs with a good sense of what rank-and-file members would tolerate decided. But it also reflected the belief among many members that they had to go along to get along.

One consequence of the strong committee system was the existence of iron triangles similar to what Shiozaki notes in Japan. Congressional committees, federal agencies, and interest groups formed three-way alliances of mutual cooperation. Centralization of power within congressional committees was crucial to the iron triangles because without it, no one in Congress could deliver the legislative support that the other two arms of the triangle needed.

THE DECENTRALIZED CONGRESS

The tradition of centralized congressional decision making came under attack in the early 1970s (see Deering and Smith 1981; Dodd and

Oppenheimer 1977; Rohde 1974; Smith and Deering 1984). The challenge was a reflection of both internal and external pressures. Many legislators, especially in the House, chafed against the tremendous power of the committee chairs. Some wanted to increase the potential for gaining political credit with their constituents through committee work. Others were like the *seisaku shinjinrui*—they had policy expertise and interests and wanted a greater say in policymaking.

Regional and ideological rivalries also played a role. Democrats from northern and western states bridled at the disproportionate number of committee chairs held by conservative southern Democrats. Southerners dominated the committee chairs because they had been elected at a young age, had never faced serious electoral challenges because they came from essentially one-party states, and thus had gained substantial seniority.

The American public aided the reformists' cause. Much as the Japanese public has become disillusioned in recent years by the Diet's inability to address the country's pressing economic woes, many Americans were deeply disillusioned by the course of the Vietnam War. They began electing more individualistic members of Congress. Like the *seisaku shinjinrui*, these new legislators were more interested in what the voters thought than what party elders thought. They were not interested in entering into an apprenticeship while more senior members managed the business of Congress. And just as Katō Kōichi of the LDP and Kan Naoto of the Democratic Party of Japan (DPJ) aided the *seisaku shinjinrui* in the battle over the Financial Revitalization Law, senior congressional Democrats who sympathized with the new legislators' policy objectives—and who also saw a chance to increase their own power—encouraged their efforts to change the way Congress did business.

The new, more individualistic members of Congress devoted much of their effort to fighting—and usually losing—battles over the substance of policy. But they also devoted a good deal of their effort to another battle, which was to rewrite the basic rules of how Congress operates.

The House eventually adopted several key reforms in the 1970s. The most important came in 1973 when the House Democratic Caucus adopted its Subcommittee Bill of Rights. The new rules stripped committee chairs of the power to make subcommittee assignments and mandated that subcommittees have formal jurisdictions, authority to hold hearings, and a staff selected by the subcommittee chair. To enforce its will, the House Democratic Caucus removed committee chairs who resisted the reforms and replaced them with members who accepted the will of the caucus.

The Senate similarly adopted several rule changes in the 1970s that decentralized power (Ornstein, Peabody, and Rohde 1977; Sinclair 1989; Smith and Deering 1984, 48–50). First, it limited senators to serving on only one of the Senate's top four committees, which included appropriations, armed services, finance, and foreign relations. This enabled junior senators to sit on the most prestigious committees earlier in their careers. The Senate subsequently increased the size of the legislative staff that junior senators could hire for their committee work. Later it barred senators from chairing more than one subcommittee per committee and made it easier for junior senators to get better subcommittee assignments.

In addition to changing the rules governing subcommittees, reformers sought to strengthen their ability to influence policy by expanding congressional staff. Many of the new staffers handled constituent problems and worked in district or state offices rather than in Washington, D.C. But many were policy experts hired to help members evaluate legislation and research issues. The number of House committee staff nearly tripled from 702 in 1970 to 1,909 in 1979, while the number of Senate staff went from 635 to 1,269 over the same period (Ornstein, Mann, and Malbin 2000, 135).

Reformers also strengthened Congress's institutional capacity for policy analysis in a bid to negate, at least in part, the decided advantage of the executive branch in policy information and expertise. The staff of the General Accounting Office, Congress's main watchdog agency, and the Congressional Research Service, which provides Congress with basic reference information, rose sharply. Congress also created two new support agencies: the Congressional Budget Office provided independent and ostensibly nonpartisan analysis of federal programs, and the Office of Technology Assessment advised Congress on scientific matters. (The latter was abolished in 1995, when Republicans won control of both houses of Congress.)

More Democratic, But Better?

These reforms of the 1970s fundamentally changed the way Congress did business. Most notable was the dispersal of power to a broader array of members. Committee chairs remained as powerful actors, but the days when a few "old bulls"—or "gurus" in Shiozaki's parlance—could run Capitol Hill as they wanted were over. The main beneficiary of this dispersal of power was subcommittee chairs—or the smaller gurus. The House, for instance, now has more than eighty subcommittee chairs. Many of them are junior members, and they wield considerable influence. As former Representative Morris Udall once joked, "We've got so many committees and subcommittees now that if you can't remember somebody's name, you just say 'Hi, Mr. Chairman'" (Davidson and Oleszek 1990, 218).

The decentralizing trend effectively weakened the power of committees. Members of Congress unwilling to defer to old bulls on their own committees were even less inclined to rubber stamp the decisions made by those on other committees. The result was that the number of amendments offered on the floor, and the number accepted, increased dramatically (Smith 1989). More members, and certainly more junior members, had gained the ability to influence congressional decision making than had ever been the case during the days of the centralized Congress.

Iron triangles also became a victim of congressional decentralization. Committees became less able to deliver the support of their parent chambers, undermining one of the prerequisites of the traditional pattern of mutual cooperation. The tremendous rise in the number of organized interest groups—which placed competing demands on committees—further undermined the system. The result was less structured, more ad hoc policymaking arrangements, called variously issue networks and "hollow-core" policymaking, that allowed greater participation (see Heclo 1978; Heinz, Laumann, Nelson, and Salisbury 1993). These new policymaking arrangements are marked by more conflictual interactions and less predictable policy decisions (Ricci 1993).

All of these developments made Congress much more democratic as an institution. It is less clear that they produced better government. While giving more people a chance to have their say about policy made the process more reflective of the views found in the country as a whole, it also made it much harder to pass major pieces of legislation. Whereas the agreement of a few old gurus once was enough for a bill to pass, today it is essential to recruit a large number of smaller gurus. Moreover, decentralization may have made it easier to pass legislation tailored to narrow interests. Because decentralization means more people have an opportunity to stop legislation, it creates more opportunities for members to hold major legislation hostage until their specific, and often unrelated, demands are satisfied.

In a way, much of the tinkering with congressional rules in the 1980s and 1990s was meant to curb the excesses of the decentralizing trend of the 1970s. Over the past two decades, Congress has sought to *re*central- ize some, but by no means all, power in the hands of party leaders (see Dodd and Oppenheimer 1989). This was especially true in the budget battles of the 1980s, when legislation such as Gramm-Rudman con- centrated power in the hands of relatively few people (see Dodd and Oppenheimer 1993; Quirk 1992). Still, Congress has not returned to the days of the old bulls, and the strains of decentralization and recentrali- zation continue to coexist somewhat uncomfortably.

SHIOZAKI'S PROPOSED REFORMS

Decentralization of congressional decision making in the 1970s proved to be a double-edged sword. That lesson is worth remembering in as- sessing Shiozaki's proposals for improving Japan's policymaking proc- ess. His hope is to ensure that the Diet will "no longer be a mere rubber stamp of bureaucrat-made policy." To that end, he proposes establish- ing a year-round Diet session and a tax council, increasing the personal staff of the prime minister and minister-level politicians, and increasing the transparency of policymaking. Another reform proposal, though implicit rather than explicit, is that the Diet learn to harness the policy interests and expertise of the *seisaku shinjinrui*.

For Americans accustomed to year-long congressional sessions and congressional staffers so numerous they constitute a fourth branch of government, none of Shiozaki's proposals is remarkable. Yet while these reforms may be needed in the Japanese context, the American experi- ence suggests their consequences may be uneven. True, they may make the Diet better able to challenge the bureaucracy. But that is not the same as restoring the control tower that Shiozaki longs for in Japanese politics.

The fact is, structural reforms by themselves do not, and cannot, create a political consensus. That task rests with society itself. And in the absence of consensus, reforms that democratize the political proc- ess will almost invariably give life to disagreements and complicate policymaking. That in itself is not bad. One responsibility of democratic governments is to air differences of policy opinion. But democratization

creates the possibility, as the American experience shows, that government by smaller political gurus may not disappear but become entrenched.

BIBLIOGRAPHY

Congressional Record. 1969. 91st Congress, 1st session. 115, pt. 21: 28156.

Davidson, Roger H., and Walter J. Oleszek. 1990. *Congress and Its Members.* 3d ed.
Washington, D.C.: Congressional Quarterly Press.

Deering, Christopher J., and Steven S. Smith. 1981. "Majority Party Leadership in
the New House Subcommittee System." In Frank H. Mackaman, ed. *Understanding Congressional Leadership.* Washington, D.C.: Congressional Quarterly
Press.

Dodd, Lawrence C., and Bruce I. Oppenheimer. 1977. "The House in Transition."
In Lawrence C. Dodd and Bruce I. Oppenheimer, eds. *Congress Reconsidered.*
New York: Praeger.

————. 1989. "Consolidating Power in the House: The Rise of the New Oligarchy."
In Lawrence C. Dodd and Bruce I. Oppenheimer, eds. *Congress Reconsidered.*
4th ed. Washington, D.C.: Congressional Quarterly Press.

————. 1993. "Maintaining Order in the House: The Struggle of Institutional
Equilibrium." In Lawrence C. Dodd and Bruce I. Oppenheimer, eds. *Congress
Reconsidered.* 5th ed. Washington, D.C.: Congressional Quarterly Press.

Heclo, Hugh. 1978. "Issue Networks and the Executive Establishment." In Anthony
King, ed. *The New American Political System.* Washington, D.C.: American
Enterprise Institute Press.

Heinz, John P., Edward O. Laumann, Robert L. Nelson, and Robert H. Salisbury.
1993. *The Hollow Core: Private Interests in National Policy Making.* Cambridge:
Harvard University Press.

Lindsay, James M. 1991. *Congress and Nuclear Weapons.* Baltimore: Johns Hopkins
University Press.

Matthews, Donald R. 1960. *U.S. Senators and Their World.* New York: Vintage.

Ornstein, Norman J., Thomas E. Mann, and Michael J. Malbin. 2000. *Vital Statistics on Congress, 1990–2000.* Washington, D.C.: American Enterprise Institute
Press.

Ornstein, Norman J., Robert L. Peabody, and David W. Rohde. 1977. "The
Changing Senate: From the 1950s to the 1970s." In Lawrence C. Dodd and
Bruce I. Oppenheimer, eds. *Congress Reconsidered.* New York: Praeger.

Quirk, Paul J. 1992. "Structure and Performance: An Evaluation." In Roger H.
Davidson, ed. *The Postreform Congress.* New York: St. Martin's Press.

Ricci, David M. 1993. *The Transformation of American Politics.* New Haven: Yale
University Press.

Rohde, David W. 1974. "Committee Reform in the House of Representatives and the Subcommittee Bill of Rights." *Annals of Political Science* 411(January): 39–47.

Sinclair, Barbara. 1989. *The Transformation of the U.S. Senate.* Baltimore: Johns Hopkins University Press.

Smith, Steven S. 1989. *Call to Order.* Washington, D.C.: Brookings Institution.

Smith, Steven S., and Christopher J. Deering. 1984. *Committees in Congress.* Washington, D.C.: Congressional Quarterly Press.

White, William S. 1956. *Citadel.* New York: Harper & Row.

8

Money and Politics in Japan

Taniguchi Masaki

EVEN since the political reforms of the 1990s, scandals have remained commonplace in Japanese politics. Here is a brief list:

- Nakajima Yōjirō, a former Defense Agency parliamentary vice-minister, received bribes of ¥5 million from Fuji Heavy Industries and submitted false financial statements on the use of political party subsidies he had misappropriated;
- Nakao Eiichi, a former minister of construction, received bribes of ¥60 million from Wakachiku Construction for his campaign expenditures;
- Yamamoto Jōji, a former representative of the Democratic Party of Japan (DPJ), swindled over ¥25 million from the government by the fictitious employment of policy staff;
- Murakami Masakuni, a former minister of labor and one of the Liberal Democratic Party (LDP) leaders in the House of Councillors, received bribes from KSD, a foundation for small- and medium-sized enterprises, as well as illegal support for his re-election.

What these scandals show is that regulation of political funding alone cannot reduce the expense of Japanese politics or the problems associated with it. More money is spent on politics in Japan than in other industrialized countries. Only the United States comes close to spending as much, both countries having candidate-centered electoral systems. In Japan, the differences among parties are vague, and each candidate is obliged to fund his personal campaign organization. The pressure to raise large sums leads some candidates astray. But the expense of Japanese politics is just a symptom of its disease, which is the state of party politics. Focusing only on political funding is to focus only on the symptom.

Before the political reforms, however, one could not even diagnose the symptom. One could only make guesses based upon hints revealed by journalists. With the new Political Fund Control Law and the introduction of the party subsidy system, the problem of Japanese politics from the perspective of money can finally be examined.

THE HISTORY OF THE POLITICAL FUNDING SYSTEM

Regulation of political funding after World War II occurred first in March 1946 with the Ministry of Home Affairs ordinance known as On the Reporting of Election Campaign Spending. According to the ordinance, candidates in the House of Representatives general election that year were to submit statements on campaign spending every seven days after announcement of the election. Similar edicts and ordinances were issued for elections of the House of Councillors and local assemblies.

Today, all candidates are required by the Public Office Election Law of 1950 to make their campaign spending public. Yet, since the limit of the campaign spending is calculated by the number of electorates in the district, candidates deliberately distinguish between expenditures for their campaign and expenditures for daily political activities. In fact, most *sebumi* activities (which take place before the official campaign period) are not included in campaign expenditures, rendering any regulation or analysis based on campaign expenditures alone meaningless.

Legal oversight of campaign spending in Japan was first enacted in the Political Fund Control Law in July 1948. This legal provision continued until the 1975 amendment of the law, which made all political funding as well as campaign spending open to public scrutiny. The emphasis of this law, however, was not regulation but disclosure, and the law was full of loopholes (Fujita 1980):

- The relationship between politicians and reported political groups was not made known;
- If a political group accepted a donation as its membership fee, the name and address of the donor were not required;
- As most spending of political groups was directed to internal sub-groups, actual spending remained unknown;
- Of political groups required to submit financial statements to the Ministry of Home Affairs, only 50 percent did so, and of groups required to submit statements to the prefectural Election Administration Commission, only about 40 percent responded;
- The supervising offices—that is, the Ministry of Home Affairs and the prefectural Election Administration Commission—lacked authority to investigate political groups;
- There was no format for reporting expenditures, and the financial statement of one political group could not be compared with that of another group;
- The definition of political group was so vague that "political parties" numbered as many as four thousand, including *habatsu* (factions) and *kōenkai* (personal election committees).

Despite the Election System Council's five attempts to reform the guidelines for political funding between 1961 and 1967, enactment of new laws was elusive. Only after the public expressed fury at revelations of the role of former Prime Minister Tanaka Kakuei in the Lockheed scandal—he was charged with accepting ¥500 million in bribes—did the government move to amend the Political Fund Control Law in 1975. For a quarter of a century, Japanese politicians had been content to leave problems as they were.

The focus of the amendment of the Political Fund Control Law was to control the direct flow of political money. Three significant changes were instituted: registration of political groups, disclosure, and regulation of donations (Iwai 1990).

Concerning the first change, the 1975 Political Fund Control Law defined six kinds of political groups, requiring all to be accountable to either the Ministry of Home Affairs or the prefectural Election Administration Commission. By this measure, the actual activities of political groups were to be now stipulated. As regards disclosure, the new law compelled all political parties and political groups to submit financial statements in a specified format. If a political group neglected to fulfill this responsibility twice, it would lose its status as a political group;

accordingly, the submission rate of financial statements rose dramatically to 90 percent.

But the most important change was the regulation of donations. The 1948 Political Fund Control Law did not limit the amount of political donations as long as they were reported in the financial statements. Politicians were therefore free to enjoy cozy relationships with companies. To prevent such abuses, the 1975 Political Fund Control Law set limits on the political donations that a company or an individual could make within a year. Companies and trade unions could donate no more than ¥150 million a year (¥100 million to political parties and individual politicians, and ¥50 million to other political groups, such as factions). Also, there was a ceiling put on each donation: companies or individuals could donate no more than ¥1.5 million to one political group or politician.

Although the 1975 Political Fund Control Law removed many loopholes, it still contained glaring defects. If the donation did not exceed ¥1 million, political groups were not required to disclose a donor's name and address. There was, furthermore, no limit on the number of political groups a donor could give to. Politicians thus could receive a large sum of money and yet mask the donor's identity. Consider the following example: Company X wants to donate ¥10 million to Politician Y. If Politician Y set up ten political groups and each accepted ¥1 million from Company X, Politician Y had no obligation to report Company X's name in the financial statements of his ten political groups.

The other problem was fundraising events, which were rampant and eluded the limits placed on political donations. Since there was no regulation regarding fundraising events, the admission price of tickets to these events became a way to make an undocumented contribution. The price of tickets rose rapidly, but unlike political donations, they were taxable, thus causing people to grumble.

With the Recruit scandal in the late 1980s, there was call for further reform of the political funding system. To obtain favorable consideration of measures relating to employment concerns, the Recruit Co., Ltd., whose business was providing personnel to corporations, distributed unlisted shares of the stock of its subsidiary, Recruit Cosmos, to specific politicians. Recipients included not only influential members of the LDP but also opposition leaders and bureaucrats. An outraged public saw the capital gains of these shares, after the stock was brought to market, as the equivalent of a bribe. Although only two politicians were arrested for their role in the scandal, others who had accepted contributions in the form of Recruit shares—including Prime Minister Takeshita Noboru and Minister of Finance Miyazawa Kiichi—bore the brunt of public criticism. In the 1989 election for the House of Councillors, the LDP lost its majority for the first time in thirty years.

To ease the public's anger, the government and the LDP began to look into political reform. Organizations like the Wise Men's Committee on Political Reform and the LDP Political Reform Committee were set up in January 1989. After discussions in these two organizations, the Eighth Election System Council drafted a series of measures that the government of Kaifu Toshiki introduced to the Diet as political reforms: an amendment to the Public Office Election Law to change the electoral system, an amendment to the Political Fund Control Law, and a bill to enact the Political Party Subsidy Law.

Election system reform split the LDP in the early 1990s, leading to the overthrow of the LDP administrations of Kaifu and Miyazawa. Under Hosokawa Morihiro's non-LDP coalition government in 1994, the bills for political reform finally passed the Diet. Except as regards the forbidding of company donations, opposition to reform of the political funding system proved to be less fierce than opposition to reform of the election system, which continued to be a source of serious contention. Laws governing the political funding system in Japan today, such as prohibiting gifts from politicians on ceremonial occasions and expanding the guilt-by-association rule (as will be discussed later), were also introduced in the 1990s.

CURRENT POLITICAL FUNDING SYSTEM

Under the 1994 Political Fund Control Law, monetary and other contributions to individual politicians by other than political parties are forbidden. Companies may not make donations to political groups other than political parties, *seiji shikin dantai* (political funding groups specified by political parties), and *shikin kanri dantai* (fundraising groups specified by politicians). (Under the 1999 amendment to the law, *shikin kanri dantai* are prohibited from accepting company donations as well.) Each politician is allowed to set up only one fundraising group.

Fundraising events are also now regulated, and steps have been taken toward greater transparency by lowering the minimum donation required for disclosure from ¥1 million to ¥50,000. Thus, in the above example of Company X and Politician Y, a large loophole has been closed. Since only one fundraising group of Politician Y can legally receive donations from Company X under the new law, Company X cannot donate more than ¥500,000 to Politician Y. Even if Politician Y chose to hold a fundraising event, a company donation that ostensibly would have been for tickets to the events could not exceed ¥1.5 million. Moreover, since all donations over ¥50,000 and tickets to events over ¥200,000 would be disclosed in Politician Y's financial statements, Company X could no longer donate more funds without anyone's knowing.

To compensate for the diminished donations and to promote the healthy development of political party activities, a political party subsidy system was introduced. That is, so as to circumvent the cultivation of cozy relationships between companies and political parties, the government granted subsidies to political parties that had a minimum of five members in the Diet or that had obtained over 2 percent of the vote in the previous election. Approximately ¥30 billion (¥250 per capita) was distributed, divided according to each party's share of votes and Diet seats.

Concerning election campaigns, the guilt-by-association rule was expanded. Previously, a candidate's culpability for corrupt practices within his campaign was limited to the acts of his executive campaign manager, chief cashier, local campaign managers, relatives, and secretaries. According to the new Public Office Election Law, the acts of lower level managers were also included in this rule. If determined to be guilty by association, a candidate would find his election invalidated and he would be prohibited from running for the office in the same district for five years. Further, to ensure its effectiveness, the law stipulated that judgment be rendered in such cases within one hundred days.

Measuring Political Funds

Under the new political funding system, how much money are political parties and politicians allowed to collect, and in what ways can they use these funds? As explained above, political groups were required to register at either the Ministry of Home Affairs or a prefectural Election

Administration Commission, depending on their geographical activity. The financial statement reported to the Ministry of Home Affairs constituted the national part of political funding, while the statement to the prefectural Election Administration Commission constituted the local part of political funding.

By summing both financial statements, the total amount reported in 1997 was ¥307 billion, triple the amount reported twenty years earlier. This rapid rise in political funds is notable as, in this same period, the consumer price index did not even double.

In 1996, the Japanese Communist Party (JCP) collected the most funds of all political parties: ¥30.4 billion. Following were the LDP at ¥26 billion; the Kōmeitō (Clean Government Party), ¥13.1 billion; the New Frontier Party (NFP), ¥12.2 billion; the Social Democratic Party (SDP), ¥9.7 billion; and the DPJ, ¥4.1 billion.

The larger part of the JCP's revenue was proceeds from its daily bulletin, *Akahata* (Red Flag). In any case, these figures reflected only the economics of the headquarters of each party. As regards the LDP, its main arena of activity was the party's local branches and election committees for representatives. If the economics of the local branches and the election committees were included in the above figures, the LDP would certainly be at the top. The DPJ, the third largest party in the House of Representatives, was sixth in rank since it was only founded in September 1996. Its largest source of revenue was its debt to the Hatoyama brothers, Yukio and Kunio, primary promoters of the DPJ.

Under the new law, the sources of LDP revenue changed dramatically. In 1996, its largest income was the political party subsidy; ten years earlier, it had been donations from companies and individuals. While this trend may be seen at the headquarters level, it is more prominent among other parties, which have fewer affiliated companies and groups. For example, the NFP, which was the second largest party in the Diet, depended on the subsidy for about 80 percent of its revenue. This development follows what occurred in Sweden, where even the most bourgeois parties virtually stopped accepting company donations after the introduction of party subsidies in 1965.

Notwithstanding these changes in political revenue, the composition of the LDP's political spending has not altered greatly. There has been a minor increase in grants to local branches, stemming from the political party subsidy delivered to the headquarters. This can also be seen in the NFP, DPJ, and SDP, where the subsidy has substituted for the limited donations given to individual politicians. The JCP, on the other hand, has refused to accept the political party subsidy, claiming that it would lead to government intervention. The organizational expenditure, which is largest in the LDP, includes a grant for the candidates endorsed for representatives and a bonus to Diet members. In 1996, LDP Diet members accepted an average of ¥12 million each.

As regards fundraising by politicians, a 1999 study by Sasaki, Yoshida, Taniguchi, and Yamamoto documented the activities of 384 representatives who won their seats in the 1996 general election, including 84 representatives who had lost but were "revived" through proportional representation.

As a rule, a politician is able to set up the following three kinds of political groups:

- one fundraising group, to which companies can donate no more than ¥500,000 a year;
- local party branches, whose presidents are concerned politicians; and
- personal election committees, to which companies cannot donate.

By specifying the groups, summing their financial statements, and offsetting the donations among them (because they are counted as income twice), the study calculated the substantial amount of each politician's revenues and expenditures. The average income of LDP representatives was ¥131.72 million, while that of NFP representatives was ¥108 million and that of DPJ representatives was ¥40.02 million. In the LDP, fundraising groups were the core organization, collecting 57 percent of revenue; in contrast, in the NFP district party branches earned 53 percent of revenue.

The fact that the revenue of about half of the NFP branches depended on grants from the headquarters suggests the NFP's party-centered electoral strategy. In comparison, since the DPJ, which was founded in September 1996, could not establish many branches in that year, the revenue of DPJ representatives was inevitably candidate-centered. (Even in January 1998, the DPJ had only 126 branches, while the LDP had 5,642 branches.)

Since party branches are able to accept company donations of more than ¥500,000, politicians will determine which purse to put the funds into, depending on the size of the donation. Large donations over ¥500,000 are to be made to political party branches, and smaller donations go to fundraising groups. Also, LDP and NFP representatives often hold fundraising events to make up for shortfalls. For personal election committees that cannot accept company donations, fundraising events provide a reliable resource, as does the transferred income from fundraising groups and political party branches.

The data in 1997 were as follows: The average income of LDP representatives was ¥105.54 million (fundraising groups, 66 percent; party branches, 23 percent; election committees, 11 percent). For NFP representatives the average income was ¥60.92 million (fundraising groups, 63 percent; party branches, 28 percent; election committees, 9 percent), and for DPJ representatives it was ¥33.16 million (fundraising groups, 75 percent; party branches, 15 percent; election committees, 11 percent). The DPJ had been working to establish its party branches, which accounts for the increase in percentage; in contrast, with the LDP and NFP, the share of the party branches decreased. The income of NFP branches showed a 70 percent decrease from the previous year, which reflects NFP's circumstances at the time: successive secessions and its dissolution in December (*Asahi Shimbun* 31 August and 1 September 1999).

The example of the political revenue received by the late Prime Minister Obuchi Keizō in 1996 is a case in point. Like other Diet members, Obuchi controlled three kinds of political groups: the fundraising group of the Society for the Study of Future Industries; the party branches of the LDP Fifth District Branch of Gunma and the LDP Hometown Development Promotion Branch; and the election committees of Keishin Kai and the Election Committee for Obuchi Keizō. The Society for the Study of Future Industries seemed to be the core organization in Tokyo, while the Election Committee for Obuchi Keizō managed other groups in Obuchi's district in Gunma Prefecture.

Since the Election Committee for Obuchi Keizō could not receive donations from companies, large amounts of money were transferred into it from Obuchi's fundraising group and LDP branches. Notably, the entire revenue of ¥43 million of the LDP Hometown Development Promotion Branch, whose ordinary expenses were zero, was transferred to the Election Committee for Obuchi Keizō and to Obuchi himself (for election campaign costs, which is legal). At the time of its founding, the Hometown Development Promotion Branch listed as its address the same address as Obuchi's office in Takasaki—a testament to its role as a dummy organization to collect donations from companies.

Evaluation of Political Funding System Reform

How can the political funding system reform in the 1990s be best evaluated? If one looks at improvements, it is apparent that corrupt practices were drastically decreased by the expanded guilt-by-association rule. According to a November 1996 survey by the *Asahi Shimbun*, 321 of 471 representatives reported that campaign spending had been reduced under the new election and political funding system.

By limiting the number of political groups that can accept company donations, the relationship between politicians and reported political groups has become much clearer. Consider again the case of Company X and Politician Y. Nine of the ten political groups that Politician Y set up to accept anonymous donations from Company X under the 1975 Political Fund Control Law—known as *yūrei dantai* (ghost groups) because they had the same office, the same clerks, and no substance—lost their utility and were dissolved.

This reform had further influence on the activities of factions of the LDP. Since factions are not classified as political parties or fundraising groups, they are no longer able to collect donations from companies and distribute the funds to their members. To get around this regulation, the fundraising groups of the leaders of each faction often distribute money to the junior members. This development can be viewed as either the degeneration of highly institutionalized faction politics in the 1980s or the generation of "leadership PACs [political action committees]" in Japan. As one ex-prime minister himself conceded to the author, faction leaders could no longer force their members to accept factional decisions through the power of money. A result of this is the ongoing pluralization of the LDP's factions.

The transparency of political funds—how much politicians receive from whom—has increased since the disclosure threshold was lowered from ¥1 million to ¥50,000. For example, former LDP Representative Yosano Kaoru's political groups—the LDP First District Branch of Tokyo and Shunzan Kai (Yosano's fundraising group)—received donations of approximately ¥57 million in 1996. Of this amount, the names and addresses of donors for over ¥49 million were made public in financial statements. If the disclosure requirements of the 1975 Political Fund Control Law had been applied, Yosano would have needed only to disclose donations amounting to ¥8.5 million. In this case, the transparency brought by the amendment afforded about six times greater visibility.

However, problems remain unresolved, even as new problems are revealed. As was the case with Obuchi's LDP Hometown Development Promotion Branch, local party branches often function as a way around the regulation of company donations. Especially in conservative parties, the money collected by party branches is usually used not for promotion of the party but for the activities of individual politicians. This "soft money" takes advantage of the gap between the concept of party-centered reform and the actual circumstances of party branches.

Also, like the LDP Hometown Development Promotion Branch, when the funds collected at a party branch are transferred to another political group, such as a fundraising group (or vice versa), a party branch functions in a money-laundering capacity by masking the real relationship between income and expenditure. Yet, to limit political party activities by law may be unconstitutional. If that is proven to be the case, consolidated accounts of each politician's groups—fundraising groups, party branches, and election committees—should be introduced to disclose the substance of money flow.

The system of disclosure for political funding remains far from foolproof. Many representatives file financial statements of their fundraising group with the Ministry of Public Management, Posts and Telecommunications, while their party branches file their statements with the prefectural Election Administration Commission. If the public wished to look at these statements, travel to each of the forty-seven prefectures would be necessary. There is no central institution—and no computerization of the system—that can serve as a clearinghouse for financial disclosure. Furthermore, the receipts that are the basis of the financial statements are unavailable for examination. The scandal surrounding Nakajima Yōjirō did not surface until an ex-secretary blew the whistle on him for false receipts in his financial statements. But with such information systematically kept from the public, suspicion and cynicism regarding politics in Japan persist.

Some Implications

What do these changes portend for what might be called the "Y2K problem" in the Japanese political funding system? Article 9 of the supplementary provision of the 1994 Political Fund Control Law stipulates:

"A measure to forbid donations by companies, trade unions, and other groups to fundraising groups will be taken five years after enforcement of this law."

Although the prohibition on company donations was opposed by some members of the LDP, the decision by Prime Minister Obuchi, in tandem with pressure brought to bear by other political parties, made the prohibition a part of the law in January 2000. As admirable as the intent may have been, however, this amendment has wrought its opposite effect.

To deal with the stringency of the amendment, the LDP subdivided its local branches so that LDP members of a prefectural or municipal assembly would be able to accept company donations. With this loophole, the only change created by the amendment was a repainting of the signboard of local fundraising groups to identify themselves as local party branches. The prohibition on company donations was thus only nominal, and the effectiveness of the overall regulation has been hampered.

Moreover, the much-sought-after goal of transparency was eroded. Because of the measures taken by the LDP, the number of party local branches will increase drastically. In the city of Shizuoka, for example, which constitutes the first district of the House of Representatives, four more LDP branches for members of the prefectural assembly will be established. With the existing two LDP branches—LDP First District Branch of Shizuoka for a candidate for the House of Representatives and LDP Shizuoka City Branch managed by members of the Shizuoka municipal assembly—there now can be six party branches in the city, each free to accept company donations.

Although a party has the right to organize itself as it sees fit, a party with such an excess of atomized, individually owned branches does not deserve to be a public institution. Nor is there a limit to the number of party branches a politician can form, or an obligation to identify which branch he controls. If a politician establishes a party branch in the name of someone else (for example, a spouse, secretary, or supporter), the opportunity to shield the true nature of political spending from the public increases.

If politicians feel the need to accept donations from companies, they should persuade the public of this fact. The goal of political funding system reform is not to abolish political funding but to enforce an accountability of political activities. Pretending to agree to the prohibition on company donations while enjoying its loopholes is not responsible political behavior. This lack of accountability is in no small way reason for the current distrust of politics. While fears of a Y2K computer problem passed without serious incident, the Y2K problem of the Japanese political funding system festers and awaits resolution.

BIBLIOGRAPHY

Fujita Hiroaki. 1980. *Nihon no seiji to kane* (Japanese politics and money). Tokyo: Keiso Shobo Service Center.

Iwai Tomoaki. 1990. *Seiji shikin no kenkyū: Rieki yūdō no Nihon-teki seiji fūdo* (A study on political funding: The Japanese climate of interest politics). Tokyo: Nihon Keizai Shimbunsha.

Sasaki Takeshi, Yoshida Shin'ichi, Taniguchi Masaki, and Yamamoto Shūji. 1999. *Daigishi to kane: Seiji shikin zenkoku chōsa hōkoku* (Representatives and money: Report on the national political funding research). Tokyo: Asahi Shimbunsha.

9

Managing the Problems of Political Finance

Thomas E. Mann

ONEY plays a problematic role in the politics of every democracy, but the "money politics" system long associated with Japan is widely viewed as a particularly virulent form. Major scandals have rocked the highest levels of Japanese politics in recent decades, revealing an unseemly scramble for political funds as well as all too frequent examples of bribery and extortion. Critics have focused primarily on the enormous sums of money flowing through the system and on the illegal actions of public officials and private actors. These certainly are major factors contributing to public distaste of politics and distrust of government, but even more troublesome is the alleged role political money has played in distorting public policies and in limiting the ability of the Japanese government to respond to changing conditions and public needs.

In his chapter, "Money and Politics in Japan," Taniguchi Masaki properly cautions against attributing too great an independent influence to political money and its regulation. He sees the powerful demand for political funds in Japan (and the problems associated with it) largely as a consequence of its candidate-centered party system, a feature it shares with the United States. Attempts to limit the supply of political funds without reducing demand are bound to generate pressures that eventually undermine both. That has been the experience in the United States since the enactment in 1974 of the first comprehensive regulatory system for campaign finance in federal elections.

Taniguchi's argument that political funding is more symptom than cause of the maladies of the Japanese political system can be extended well beyond candidate-centered elections. Money may well have been an essential lubricant in the dominant Liberal Democratic Party (LDP) political machine, but the distinctive pattern of party politics and policy-making in Japan was shaped by many powerful forces, including the single non-transferable vote (SNTV) electoral system, the mal-apportionment of Diet constituencies favoring rural interests, a strong bureaucracy, widespread consensus on national goals, and the impressive performance of the postwar economy (Curtis 1999).

Some architects and supporters of the 1994 reform of the electoral system were surprised and disappointed when the shift to a mixed-member system (with 300 single-seat districts and 200 proportional seats) failed to transform the money politics system and produce a British-style two-party competition. Surely their expectations far outpaced any reasonable calculation of the likely effects, especially in the short term, of this electoral reform (Reed and Thies 2001, 380–403; Carlson 2001). So, too, champions of political financing reforms would be unwise to expect too much from altering the laws under which politicians raise and spend political funds. Taniguchi's review of the history of political funding reform in Japan reveals no shortage of successful efforts to alter the laws but also ample evidence of the limits of those new laws in producing the desired effects. Viewed from an American perspective, this experience looks very familiar. The point is not that all funding reform is doomed to failure, but rather that any solution is perforce partial and temporary, and provides limited leverage on broader problems of governance.

PROBLEMS OF POLITICAL FUNDING

From this perspective, then, what are the major problems associated with political funding and what tools are available for managing those problems? Taniguchi emphasizes the high costs of Japanese politics and the attendant pressures to engage in corrupt activities. A more general formulation is that problems arise as candidates and parties struggle to raise resources to compete effectively when the costs have risen sharply and groups and individuals with resources seek to influence election outcomes and policy decisions. In the United States, where campaign expenditures have accelerated in recent elections, the problem is less the overall cost of elections than how political funds are raised and spent. The situation in Japan appears to be similar.

One set of concerns revolves around the linkages between private contributions and public decisions. At one extreme are bribery and extortion, explicit quid-pro-quo exchanges that violate criminal statutes. The most notorious Japanese political funding scandals fall into this category. But well short of illegal actions lie such problems as the dependence of politicians on large financial contributors, conflicts of interest between fundraising and policymaking, and the damage to democratic legitimacy from the appearance of special access and influence by political donors. A related concern is the impact of the money chase—the unending scramble for political money—on how party and public officials spend their time, whom they see and listen to, and how both affect governance.

Another set of problems is associated directly with the electoral process. Rising costs and inadequate political funding can depress electoral competition, discourage able people from seeking office, give special advantage to incumbents, political dynasties, and wealthy self-financed candidates, and weaken democratic accountability by muffling the voices of individuals, groups, candidates, and parties without sufficient resources to be heard.

POLITICAL FINANCE TOOLS

The political finance tools available to policymakers—disclosure, limits on contributions, expenditure controls, public subsidies, and regulation of campaign activity—have been used, with varying degrees of enforcement and effectiveness, in both Japan and the United States to deal with these problems (Mann 2001). Taniguchi's chronicle of the history of political funding regulation in Japan, in which early laws riddled with loopholes and routinely ignored were gradually strengthened, bears a striking resemblance to the American experience with campaign finance regulation.

Disclosure requirements for political donations and expenditures are predicated on the assumption that transparency serves as a deterrent to corruption and influence peddling. Unfortunately, such requirements often fail to produce complete and comprehensible information that is publicly available on a timely basis. That was clearly the practice in the United States for many decades until the law was changed in 1974 to set up a central agency, the Federal Election Commission, to collect and publicize reports from all federal candidates and political committees. Taniguchi demonstrates that Japan has come some way on disclosure since the loophole-ridden Political Fund Control Law of 1948. Reducing the number of political committees associated with politicians, establishing a common reporting format, lowering the threshold for reportable donations, and applying disclosure requirements to fundraising dinners have increased the level of transparency. A much higher percentage of donors are now identified by name. Yet even after the law was tightened, it took a team of scholars working many months after the election in the Ministry of Home Affairs and the forty-seven prefectural election administration committees to piece together a reasonably accurate picture of fundraising and spending by candidates and parties. The disclosure system in Japan seems designed to control information, not to disseminate it on a timely basis to the public.

CONTRIBUTION LIMITS

Limits on the sources and size of political contributions have been embraced by policymakers in both Japan and the United States. For many decades, corporations and unions in the United States have been prohibited from making contributions in federal elections, although they may form voluntary political action committees (PACs) through which to make their contributions to parties and candidates. In recent years, these restrictions have been rendered largely ineffectual through the emergence of "soft money" donations to political parties not subject to federal regulation. Contributions to candidates and parties from individuals and PACs have been limited in size since 1974. The failure to index these limits for inflation has reduced the real value of donation ceilings by more than two-thirds and intensified the money chase (see Corrado et al. 1997).

Following laws passed in 1985, 1994, and 1999, Japan has a very elaborate set of limitations governing contributors and recipients of political donations. As Taniguchi describes, company donations are now limited in size and restricted to political funding groups set up by political parties. Companies are barred from contributing to individual politicians or their fundraising groups as well as to other groups. Corporate contributions have declined, and party factions have become at most bit players in political funding, a dramatic change from the days in which Tanaka Kakuei built his "money politics" machine (Schlesinger 1997).

At the same time, the relative freedom of political party organizations from restrictions on donations, transfers, and contributions has led to a proliferation of local party branches, which serve primarily to launder company donations to politicians and to avoid disclosure. American experience with soft money contributions to parties that are used primarily for candidate-centered campaign activity suggests that the Japanese party loophole could soon render obsolete the laws governing disclosure and donations. What appear on the surface to be party-building measures are in reality means for individual politicians to avoid the strictures of the law.

SPENDING LIMITS

The U.S. Supreme Court ruled in its 1976 *Buckley v. Valeo* decision that mandatory spending limits are an unconstitutional violation of the First Amendment guarantee of free speech. Only voluntary limits tied to the acceptance of public funding were judged acceptable. For several cycles, these voluntary limits worked to restrain spending in presidential elections, but more recently party soft money and candidate-specific issue advocacy have effectively removed any constraint on spending.

Unlike the situation in the United States, where campaign finance regulations apply to entire election cycles, Japanese law draws a clear distinction between an official campaign period (presently limited to only twelve days) and the time that precedes it. Campaigns are tightly regulated. During this period candidates are prohibited from doing what their U.S. counterparts do year-round: promote themselves through television and radio advertising, direct mail, and door-to-door canvassing. Limits on expenditures during this official campaign period are also provided for by law, but the severe restrictions on campaign activity and the briefness of the formal campaign render these spending limits largely inconsequential.

Most campaigning occurs beforehand, when Diet members nurture their personal support organizations (*kōenkai*) and work to deliver benefits for their local constituencies. There are no limits on political expenditures made outside the official campaign period, so the demands on members and aspirants to raise money to build and maintain their own political machine are unrestrained. The severe restrictions on candidates during the official campaign period contribute to the expensive, personalistic political activity that Japanese politicians engage in continuously.

PUBLIC SUBSIDIES

Since acquiring adequate funding for political party operations and election campaigns is a major challenge facing all democracies, one made all the more difficult by concerns about excessive dependence on large donors, it is not surprising that public subsidies have become commonplace around the world. These subsidies take the form of direct cash assistance, the provision of goods and services, and indirect support such as tax credits or deductions for contributions.

Japan established a public subsidy for political parties in 1994, as part of a broader effort to reduce company donations and strengthen parties. These public subsidies—in combination with new transparency requirements, the 1993 decision of the Keidanren industrial federation to discontinue its longstanding practice of mediating corporate contributions to the parties, and economic difficulties and restructuring of companies—have substantially altered the revenue sources of the parties, especially the LDP.

Taniguchi documents how donations from companies and individuals now constitute a much smaller share of the LDP's income. A veteran LDP staff fundraiser reported that corporate contributions to the LDP have declined from a peak of ¥16 billion annually to ¥4 billion or ¥5 billion. The public subsidy has replaced existing party revenue, not added to it, in spite of the absence of any limits on what the parties can raise and spend (personal interview 1998).

REGULATION OF CAMPAIGN ACTIVITY

One strategy for reducing the demand for political money is to prohibit costly campaign activities. A large number of countries ban paid political advertising on television, although most couple the ban with free television time to the parties. Such prohibitions are unthinkable in the United States, where free speech guarantees preclude any significant restraint on political communication. Japan severely limits what candidates can do during the official campaign period while giving parties a much freer hand. For example, parties can circulate handbills, run political ads in newspapers and magazines, and buy time on television and radio—but, in every case, only as long as they do not mention the names of any of their candidates. As Gerald Curtis (1992, 222–243) has observed, regulations that prevent parties from advertising their candidates and candidates from advertising themselves severely constrain the use of the media as a campaign tool, yet do little to reduce the demand for political funds.

CONSEQUENCES OF REFORM

If the goals of political funding reform in Japan, coupled with the change in the electoral system, were to reduce the costs of politics, slow the money chase, eliminate corruption, weaken the linkages between private donors and policymakers, and shift the basis of electoral decisions from locally oriented candidates to nationally based and policy-differentiated parties, that reform has been a disappointment. Failure to reduce the demand for political funds by politicians has frustrated many of the most ambitious objectives of reformers.

If, on the other hand, one begins with more modest expectations, these reforms are not without some consequences, even constructive ones. Reform of the electoral system has reduced the effective number of candidates in single-member districts and strengthened efforts to consolidate opposition to the LDP in the Diet. Over time those effects might become more pronounced. Factions within the LDP play a much less significant electoral role—endorsing and funding candidates—although they continue some critical functions within government. Their links with corporate interests and the local roots of their political machines have attenuated. The extension of "guilt-by-association" provisions and more rigorous enforcement has put some teeth in election laws. Political fundraising is more transparent, although far from adequate. Public funds have replaced a large share of private donations. A higher percentage of political funds flow through the parties.

Within this more modest framework, Taniguchi believes that the Japanese soft money problem should be the primary focus of the next round of funding reform. The prohibition on company donations to politicians is being circumvented by the proliferation of local party branches entirely beholden to individual politicians. This makes a mockery of the prohibition and, by shielding information about contributors from the public, weakens accountability. Either repeal the ban on company donations to politicians or close the local party loophole, Taniguchi argues. Sounds familiar and compelling to this American student of political finance.

His recommendation raises the broader question of what approach to political funding reform makes most sense for Japan, given realistic expectations of what can be accomplished through this area alone. The history of political corruption in Japan argues against a wholesale deregulation of political finance as advocated by libertarians in the United States. The absence of a tradition of individual philanthropy in Japan extends to political giving, meaning that political fundraising is perforce dependent upon public subsidies and organized interests. Full public financing has its own serious obstacles and side effects. And further restrictions on company donations will intensify efforts to build an underground economy in political funding.

Perhaps the most promising approach is to consider measures that might reduce the demand for political funds by politicians. Deregulating and lengthening the duration of the official campaign period, while providing blocks of publicly subsidized television time to the parties, might help. If parties are free to promote their candidates, and candidates are able to utilize the wide array of communication tools to advance their campaigns, some of the pressure on individual politicians to maintain expensive year-round *kōenkai* might be relieved. Adequate public funding of Diet members' staff and office expenses would also help.

Whatever additional steps are taken, improved transparency of political funding is an essential element of reform. The money politics machine of Tanaka and his successors has been under assault on a number of fronts, but a more robust disclosure regime combined with

aggressive enforcement offers the greatest protection against falling
back into old, bad habits.

BIBLIOGRAPHY

Carlson, Matthew. 2001. "Consequences of Electoral Reform in Japan: The
    Changing Costs and Quality of Competition." Paper prepared for the American
    Political Science Association 2001 Annual Meeting, San Francisco, California.
Corrado, Anthony, et al. 1997. *Campaign Finance Reform: A Sourcebook.* Washington,
    D.C.: Brookings Institution Press (new edition forthcoming in 2002).
Curtis, Gerald L. 1992. "Japan." In David Butler and Austin Ranney, eds. *Election-
    eering: A Comparative Study of Continuity and Change.* Oxford: Clarendon
    Press.
————. 1999. *The Logic of Japanese Politics: Leaders, Institutions, and the Limits of
    Change.* New York: Columbia University Press.
Mann, Thomas E. 2001. "Political Money and Party Finance." *International En-
    cyclopedia of the Social and Behavioral Sciences* 3(11).
Reed, Steven R., and Michael F. Thies. 2001. "The Consequences of Electoral
    Reform in Japan." In Matthew Soberg Shugart and Martin P. Wattenberg,
    eds. *Mixed-Member Electoral Systems: The Best of Both Worlds?* New York: Ox-
    ford University Press.
Schlesinger, Jacob M. 1997. *Shadow Shoguns: The Rise and Fall of Japan's Postwar
    Political Machine.* New York: Simon & Schuster.

10

The Changing Shape of Party Politics and Governance in Japan

Sasaki Takeshi

I N the June 2000 general election of the House of Representatives (Lower House), the Liberal Democratic Party (LDP), despite the strong support of the New Kōmeitō (NK), lost 38 seats in single-member district elections and lost the majority in the Lower House which it had held before the election. The Democratic Party of Japan (DPJ), the largest opposition party, increased its number of seats from 95 to 127. Other opposition parties, such as the Liberal Party (LP) and the Social Democratic Party (SDP), saw small gains, but the Japanese Communist Party (JCP) sustained big losses (see table 1).

But the election of 2000 should also be viewed relative to the election of 1996. At that time, the LDP won 239 seats, representing 47.8 percent of the Lower House; because of a subsequent decrease in the total number of seats in the legislative body, the LDP's 233 seats in the year 2000 actually accounts for a larger portion—48.5 percent—of the Lower House. By a quick comparison of the two elections, the LDP would seem thereby to have increased rather than decreased its Diet presence in 2000 (see table 2).

Prior to this election, the LDP controlled a majority of 271 seats, a figure that included extra-electoral seats. The 32-seat difference can be accounted for by Diet members who defected from the New Frontier

Table 1. Results of the Lower House General Election of 2000

	Single-Member Elections		Proportional Elections		Total
	No. of Seats	% of Votes	No. of Seats	% of Votes	No. of Seats
Liberal Democratic Party	177	41	56	28.3	233
Democratic Party of Japan	80	27.6	47	25.2	127
New Kōmeitō	7	2	24	13	31
Liberal Party	4	3.4	18	11	22
Japanese Communist Party	0	12.1	20	11.2	20
Social Democratic Party	4	3.8	15	9.4	19
New Conservative Party	7	2	0	0.4	7
Others	21	7.8	0	1.5	21

Source: Asahi Shimbun 26 June 2000.

Table 2. Results of the Lower House General Election of 1996

	Single-Member Elections		Proportional Elections		Total
	No. of Seats	% of Votes	No. of Seats	% of Votes	No. of Seats
Liberal Democratic Party	169	38.6	70	32.8	239
New Frontier Party	96	28	60	28	156
Democratic Party of Japan	17	10.6	35	16.1	52
Japanese Communist Party	2	12.6	24	13.1	26
Social Democratic Party	4	2.2	11	8.4	15
Sakigake	2	1.3	0	1	2
Others	10	6.7	0	2.6	10

Source: Asahi Shimbun 21 October 1996.

Party (NFP) after 1996 and, subsequent to its dissolution, joined the LDP. Thus, the LDP can be said to have gone into the 2000 election bulked up with the extra-electoral seats, which it simply lost.

At any rate, the dissolution of the NFP complicates any analysis of the 2000 election. Former NFP members also joined the DPJ, enlarging its representation from 52 to 95, and eventually to 127. Unlike the LDP, however, the DPJ did not lose extra-electoral seats, succeeding instead in consolidating its position. Between the 1996 and 2000 elections, the DPJ increased its share of seats dramatically—from 10.4 percent to 26.4 percent. Even so, the DPJ is only a little less than half the size of the LDP, similar to the Socialist Party under the 1955 system, but the DPJ's record in the recent series of elections has been impressive.

Politically, a major topic of the 2000 election was the establishment of the LDP-NK voting coalition—a cabinet coalition that extended to voters as well. The New Kōmeitō limited the number of its candidates in single-member district elections to the number that the LDP gave up. At the same time, some LDP candidates appealed to their supporters to cast votes for the NK in proportional elections. There is no definitive analysis of how successful this controversial strategy was. An exit poll showed that 65 percent of NK supporters voted for LDP candidates and 15 percent for DPJ candidates. In districts where the election pitted an independent ex-LDP candidate against an NK candidate officially supported by the LDP, 60 percent of LDP supporters reportedly voted for the independent candidate. The data do illustrate the defection of LDP supporters, but it seems fair to say that the LDP owes its 177 seats and 40.97 percent of the total vote in single-member district elections to the support of the NK. The huge gap in LDP support between single-member elections and proportional elections—12.6 percent—indirectly confirms this relationship. On the other hand, the NK has gained enormous influence among LDP members at the sacrifice of some of its seats.

The LDP-NK coalition had its origins in the LDP's defeat in the House of Councillors (Upper House) election of 1998, which brought about the fall of the cabinet of Hashimoto Ryūtarō. Since then, LDP leaders, aware of their growing vulnerability, came to see the loyal troop of NK supporters as the only reliable partner to compensate for weakening LDP voting blocs.

Generally speaking, a coalition at the cabinet level should be clearly differentiated at the election level. But in the case of the LDP-NK coalition, the collaboration at the election level seems to have been prioritized from the very beginning. It must be recognized, however, that the LDP increased its presence by only three points in single-member district elections despite strong NK support. In the proportional elections, the LDP's share decreased from 32.8 percent to 28.3 percent. As a whole, these results suggest not only that the LDP was weaker than in 1996 but also that the LDP will not easily be able to free itself from its dependence on the NK. In the future, the LDP will face the question whether it is strong enough to go to election without considering support from the NK.

In the 2000 election, the DPJ consolidated its position as a challenger to the LDP, visualizing the possibility of a two-party system in

Japan. In single-member district elections, the LDP and the DPJ controlled 85.6 percent of total seats, with the split-ticket voting of opposition supporters clearly benefiting DPJ candidates. If the DPJ had defeated the LDP in proportional elections, the DPJ might have appeared as a de facto victor in the election. But in proportional elections, which both the LDP and DPJ were losers in, a weakness of the DPJ could be seen. According to an exit poll in the proportional elections, 26 percent of DPJ supporters voted for the SDP, the LP, and even the LDP. Thus, it is the proportional system that has contributed to the fragmentation of party support and to damaging the DPJ as well as the LDP. Put another way, neither the DPJ nor the LDP was strong enough to sweep the proportional elections.

Yet, this was good news for the DPJ. In Japan, the number of independent voters is now so large (representing about 50 percent of all voters) that every party has made serious effort to pick up their support. Independent voters consist of politically heterogeneous groups. Among these voters, an exit poll showed the DPJ to be the most supported party in both single-member district elections (38 percent versus 28 percent for the LDP) and proportional elections (37 percent versus 14 percent for the LDP). Another poll showed that 40 percent of independent voters in urban areas supported the DPJ (as opposed to 10 percent supporting the LDP); even in rural areas, 32 percent of independent voters supported the DPJ. The strength of the DPJ among independent voters was already apparent in pre-election polls that showed the DPJ as the least unfavorable party. In large cities, such as Tokyo, the DPJ has become the most popular party, several young DPJ candidates in urban areas defeating more powerful LDP candidates, including well-known ex-ministers. In fact, it was the DPJ's support from independent voters that reportedly offset the NK support of the LDP candidates. Of these results, journalists have suggested that the DPJ represents the interests of the cities and the LDP the interests of the countryside.

At the same time, exit polls have shown generational differences in support for the DPJ and the LDP. The DPJ has become the party for voters in their twenties, thirties, and forties, in contrast with the LDP, which has been most popular among people fifty and older. One poll showed strong support among men for the DPJ, while women tended to prefer the LDP—an interesting finding in that the traditional image of the LDP has been the party of men. Indeed, post-election studies have confirmed the LDP as the party of choice for farmers, housewives, and gray generations, while the DPJ has gained supporters among young, urban salarymen in their thirties and forties.

In this light, the 2000 election is more important for revealing the social cleavages among Japanese voters than for the changes in party representation in the Lower House.

Economic Crisis and Party Politics

The election of 2000, however, did not contribute much to the public policy agenda. The campaign was dominated by a series of mysterious missteps by Prime Minister Mori Yoshirō more than by concrete discussions of issues such as fiscal policy or social security.

The lack of discussion does not mean that there were no serious issues in Japanese politics. On the contrary, between 1996 and 2000, the country was enmeshed in the most serious economic crisis in the thirty years. In the election of 1996, Hashimoto, as prime minister, was given the mandate to implement a number of structural reforms, including the deregulation of the financial markets and a tax increase. In the fall of 1997, Japanese financial markets were hit by the bankruptcies of several local banks and securities firms even as financial crisis was wreaking havoc in Asia. This exacerbated the crisis in Japan, which in turn worsened the crisis in Asia. The Hashimoto cabinet, let alone the Japanese system of government, was severely tested.

The crisis marked the beginning of the decline of the Japanese bureaucracy. The turbulence in the financial markets revealed huge holes in the Ministry of Finance: it was ill-prepared to address the serious issues and it was wanting in crisis management. Forced to reconsider their tight fiscal policy and to cut taxes, the cabinet and the LDP were in near paralysis. The change of course in fiscal policy that was effected did little to solve the problems of the Japanese banking system, unemployment shot up, and the bankruptcies of big companies became an everyday affair. Amid this turbulence, Japanese began to lose the trust they had placed in politicians and bureaucrats, to doubt the fundamentals of their economic system, and to recognize that the era of enormous economic stability and growth was ending. The Upper House election of 1998 was dominated by economic concerns, and Hashimoto was unable to persuade the electorate to persevere in its support of the LDP.

The turbulence continued after Hashimoto was turned out of office.

Bureaucrats were discredited and lost their power, leaving politicians to determine a concrete formula to address the crisis of the banking system. The difficulties were not to be solved easily, and in autumn 1998 it became evident that the economic crisis and the political crisis were feeding off each other. Eventually, Obuchi Keizō, who succeeded Hashimoto as prime minister, made the decision to fight the growing crisis of credit by pouring in enormous amounts of public money. At the same time, he mobilized fiscal policy so as to generate economic growth.

Hashimoto's reform policy, which had been oriented toward spending cuts and moderate reform of the bureaucracy, was replaced by Obuchi's spend-spend policy and big-government orientation. Any credibility of the moderate reform policy mandated by the 1996 election had been destroyed by the widening financial crisis, but at the same time, the crisis created a climate where it was possible for politicians to implement bold policies that bureaucrats could have never imagined. With the breakdown of the old system and the de facto end of the bureaucracy-dominated system, *kan̄-shudō-taisei*, power shifted from the bureaucrats to the politicians. To consolidate this new power of political parties and the prime minister, the LDP agreed with Ozawa Ichirō, former leader of the NFP, to increase the number of posts in each ministry that were to be politically appointed—a politics-dominated system known as *seiji-shudō-taisei*.

To take the initiative in crisis management is one thing, but to succeed at it is something else. Most Japanese understood Obuchi's redirection of policy as necessary to cope with the crisis, and Obuchi's popularity rose steadily in 1999. But it was also clear that Obuchi's generous spend-spend policy and public credit loan system were to a large extent embodiments of the dreams of the LDP. Until then, the Ministry of Finance had controlled the budget deficit and credit system tightly, relegating politicians to the role of a pressure group. Thus, Obuchi's policy had two faces: a necessary crisis-management measure that was also the chance to realize old-fashioned policy. Obuchi was happy to reconcile the two aims, but this compatibility could not continue forever. Measures undertaken during crisis are extraordinary and temporary. Yet, the LDP wanted to enjoy this golden moment as long as possible and to establish these measures as normal—not extraordinary—policy.

Ironically, the more successful was Obuchi's policy, the more apparent became the tension underlying his orientation. The most conspicuous example was a statement in August 1999 by Katō Kōichi, ex-secretary-general of the LDP, that the time had come to stop the spend-spend policy and face the budget-deficit problem. This statement coincided with DPJ leaders' dramatizing the budget deficit and calling for a tax increase. Supporters of Obuchi's policy contended that economic growth was a necessary precondition for Japanese banks to deal with the huge amount of bad credit and for companies to correct their credit imbalances, while critics maintained that Obuchi's policy could not bring about any visible economic recovery and would simply delay the restructuring of the economic status quo. The skyrocketing increase in the budget deficit and the downgrading of Japanese bonds began to cast a gloom over the Japanese public. A poll in spring 2000, just before Obuchi was struck down by a fatal illness, indicated a populace split into two opposing groups as to whether the bold spending policy should be continued or whether the budget deficit should be addressed.

In the discussion of Japanese economic policy, the public works complex emerged as the main culprit of the inefficiency and waste of governmental activities. First, the weighting of this sector in the Japanese budget, in comparison with other industrialized countries, was far out of proportion to other sectors. Second, within Japan itself, as public works programs were no longer effective in encouraging growth, the weighting of the programs lost popularity. Third, public works programs were used as a policy tool to prop up construction companies that had suffered badly by the burst of the bubble economy in the 1990s. The heavy debt of these construction companies had, in large part, caused the crisis of the banking system, and public works were being used to maintain the status quo at the cost of public money. Politically, the construction industry has long been among the most important supporters of the LDP, many small construction firms having functioned as a de facto election machine for the party. Moreover, because public works also provided the economically devastated countryside with meaningful help, perpetuation of the programs was critical for the LDP, particularly before the general election.

Fourth, public works programs meant huge subsidies for the agricultural sector and the countryside, a stronghold of LDP support. In fact, it was through public works programs that the LDP government was able to transfer income from urban areas to rural areas. When the economic bubble burst and the country's financial crisis dragged on, urban voters grew less tolerant of "wasteful" public works programs and this system of income transfer. As urban voters increasingly identified the LDP with public works and rural interests, the DPJ gained ground by calling for the downsizing of public works programs.

In this context, public works programs became the dividing issue among Japanese voters. In urban areas, with the LDP losing seats and the DPJ emerging as the most popular party, election results seemed to be a reflection of the parties' stances on public works. In rural areas, DPJ candidates were met with stronger challenges than ever, with Hatoyama Yukio, president of the DPJ, barely winning over the LDP candidate in his home district in Hokkaido.

Overall, the LDP relied on its message of "stability" and the pork barrel, while the DPJ proposed the end of pork-barrel politics and the radical restructuring of the public sector. In the current national atmosphere, the traditional message of the pork barrel seemed to have less effect, given that many now believe interest politics of this kind to destabilize the future economic life of the country.

The LDP was shocked by the election results. The party had cultivated a following with huge amounts of public funds, and it had gained strong support nationwide from the NK. Until the financial crisis hit hard, the LDP had, in the face of economic downturn, benefited from an unspoken pressure among the populace to support the LDP. But as it became clear that the crisis originated from a breakdown of the postwar economic structure, which the LDP had largely crafted, the LDP's traditional measures began to lose credibility. The LDP's unpopularity among independent voters seems to be related to this point. Even though Japanese have not yet said "yes" to the DPJ, especially young people in urban areas, some have clearly begun to say "no" to the LDP.

In 1996, most Japanese still believed that Hashimoto's policies of piecemeal reform were sufficient to guide the economy through the new terrain of globalization and the information technology (IT) revolution. The more radical proposals of the NFP were not well received. With the financial and economic crises the country has undergone since 1997, however, the political landscape has changed. Hashimoto's downfall illustrated the public frustration with LDP leadership. Obuchi may have been more successful in handling crises but left behind the worst budget deficit in Japanese history. Although the number of seats won by the LDP and the DPJ were not greatly different following the 1996 and 2000 elections, economic crisis has altered the underlying political circumstances significantly.

PARTY POLITICS AND THE LEGACY OF THE
JAPANESE BUREAUCRATIC SYSTEM

Japanese have accepted a bureaucratic system operating under esoteric doctrine, while their representatives in government are decision makers acting upon exoteric—that is, constitutional—principle. The esoteric doctrine has not been identified in any document, so it has not been possible to overcome it by revising laws or amending the constitution. Postwar LDP politics depended heavily on the de facto symbiosis of the two doctrines, without institutionalizing priorities. It was a system in which the LDP protected the bureaucracy from attacks by outsiders, including the populace, while the bureaucracy provided the LDP with enormous economic success and voting blocs that the bureaucracy controlled either directly or indirectly. Until the beginning of the 1990s, if a bureaucrat referred to a political party, he was invariably referring to the LDP. This coexistence thrived as long as the bureaucracy achieved its promises.

There were two blind spots in this coexistence. The first was a change of power. When the LDP lost its majority in 1993 and the cabinet of Hosokawa Morihiro was formed, the LDP observed a bureaucracy suddenly, according to the exoteric principle, responsive to a cabinet of former opposition parties; the LDP's alliance with the bureaucracy had not been bound by anything but power dependency. The non-LDP cabinet survived only ten months, but this change of power severely damaged the postwar alliance between the LDP and the bureaucracy. Returning to power, the LDP spoke openly about its differences with the bureaucracy, even sometimes criticizing the performance of certain ministries. The brief change of power had ended the vague marriage between the esoteric and exoteric doctrines. The LDP now understood the exoteric principle as solely legitimate. A political party could not rely on the bureaucracy but must press its real will on the public by controlling the bureaucracy.

The second blind spot was the weakening effectiveness of the bureaucratic system. The Japanese bureaucratic system consolidated its extraordinary position during wartime in the 1930s and 1940s, planning and directing the national economy. The system consisted of a huge body of regulations and direct and indirect controls, so it worked well when the Japanese economic system was more or less closed and international circumstances were stable. It worked almost perfectly in the 1960s. But

Japanese economic successes destroyed these presuppositions, and the bureaucratic system had continuously to adapt its structure to pressures from the outside as well as to prove its effectiveness by showing off the "new" Japan.

Japan's trade friction with the United States in the 1980s and 1990s was significant in the weakening of what had been an air-tight bureaucratic system. One after another, bureaucrats were forced to concede to outside pressures; they could no longer control the situation. As Japanese multinational corporations reinforced their position in the world, the bureaucracy became more extraneous than helpful. Fundamentally, the Japanese bubble economy came about by the mismatch between the anachronistic bureaucratic system and the huge flow of money into the country.

Once the economic bubble burst, the bureaucracy proved fairly helpless. Unable to restructure the old system to address new national circumstances, it focused on the interests of less-competitive sectors. Consequently, in the 1990s the bureaucratic system became more of a problem than problem solver. Its respect gone, the bureaucracy found itself politically vulnerable as never before. In addition, the personal scandals of some bureaucrats further impressed on the public the understanding that bureaucrats were working for their own interests in collaborating with less-competitive sectors through wasteful public works programs. The rapid decline of bureaucratic authority was one of the most noteworthy events of the 1990s.

Thus, the 1990s also saw political parties having to face the issue of reform of the bureaucratic system. While the LDP maintained strong ties to the bureaucracy in terms of personal relationships and political mobilization, the DPJ emphasized its strong anti-bureaucratic stance. The administrative reform initiated by Hashimoto and put into force in 2001, however, was less of a radical breakthrough than a realization for politicians that bureaucratic power in the ministries could be reexamined and the system changed. In substance, it mainly lessened the number of ministries by combining them into a few, not eliminating any, and thus disrupting the deep-seated identities the old ministries had enjoyed. But the LDP did not have a plan to downsize bureaucratic powers.

During discussions on administrative reform, the Hashimoto cabinet tried simultaneously to devolve power from the central government to local governments, but Hashimoto did not support a radical devolution plan. So it seems fair to say that his reforms were exoteric in the sense that politicians could take important action with regard to the bureaucracy.

The only substantial change effected by the administrative reform was a drastic reorganization of the Prime Minister's Office. Until then, the Japanese prime minister had been surrounded, rather without choice, by bureaucrats from respective ministries. In the new system, the prime minister controls some key positions and is free to make appointments as he sees fit, whether or not they are politicians. The introduction of this appointee system has been broadly supported by the public as the first step toward controlling the bureaucratic system. Ozawa later pushed the LDP to extend this system to more ministries, so that after 2001 the government would have more ministerial positions to be filled by appointment by the prime minister. This arrangement is a politics-dominated, as opposed to a bureaucracy-dominated, system.

The political meaning of the new politics-dominated system, however, has not been sufficiently comprehended by politicians. Institutionally, Japan has sought to follow the British example, whereby the system is prime minister– or cabinet-dominated. In that sense, the governing party, and especially the LDP, must itself change to realize the desired results.

In the 1990s, Japan had eight prime ministers. The governing party or parties changed prime ministers so often that the political preconditions for meaningful leadership by a prime minister were destroyed. Each prime minister, moreover, reshuffled the cabinet almost yearly, leaving the ministers with little time to learn policy issues and to force bureaucrats to act accordingly. This political custom, begun by the LDP in the 1970s, originated with the intention to maintain peace within the party by giving each Diet member an equal chance at a ministerial post. The intra-party strategy was a comfortable arrangement for party members as well as for the bureaucrats. Everyone understood that this system could work only under the condition that the minister reigned, but did not rule. Yet, in a different day, if politicians stick to this "equality of result" principle, the new system can bring about no real change.

Another recalcitrant political custom has been at work. In the scenario where the minister has essentially been a dummy, it has not been the cabinet that has made policy decisions. Instead, the actual decision making has been done by politicians in the governing party working closely with the bureaucrats. This intimate coalition effectively limited any substantial policy role for the prime minister or his cabinet. Consequently, the secretary-general of a party and the chairman of the party's policy research council, in particular, have wielded more power than have the ministers or even the prime minister. Bureaucrats alone could not usurp the decision-making authority, but neither could politicians without the partnership of bureaucrats. Together they ruled.

The problem with such an arrangement is the fragmentation of policies and the poverty of integration. Each ministry pursues its own policies under its institutional purview, resulting in innumerable, fragmented bureaucracy-dominated systems; there is no one bureaucracy-dominated system. If the politicians are similarly satisfied with addressing policy in fragmented ways, they can be characterized as "bureaucratized" politicians. If they wish to become real politicians, they need to free themselves from bureaucratic fragmentation and be prepared to undertake the responsibility of integrated policymaking.

But it is not clear that the politicians will agree to this change in the political game. The tradition of *tō-shudō-taisei,* the governing party–dominated system, is a way of political life, and politicians in the governing party have long devoted a great deal of energy pressing the demands of their constituencies on bureaucrats. For many politicians, the pressure they bring to bear on bureaucrats—and the compromises they extract—is politics itself or, certainly, politics as usual.

The Diet enacted a law that punished politicians who pressured bureaucrats and received money from their constituency as a reward for doing so. Despite this legal restriction, the political game continues. Nor is the situation aided by the fact that bureaucrats are leery of political appointments—in particular, Diet members serving as vice-ministers or policy advisors—who would sooner interfere in the bureaucracy with the specific demands of their constituencies than concentrate on policymaking. At any rate, it is urgent that there be further laws controlling contact between politicians and bureaucrats, but thus far no party has shown sufficient resolve in doing so.

What the country needs is less fragmented, more strategic, more systematic government in policymaking and implementation. Unless there are fundamental changes to the political game that most politicians in the Japanese parliamentary system play, public disillusionment will only grow worse. The country has tired of the old rhetoric bashing bureaucrats. It is time for Japanese politics to govern.

In Search of a New Style of Governance

The old style of Japanese governance was clearly on the brink of collapse by the end of the twentieth century. The old style has been described as a collaboration between the public sector (the bureaucracy) and the private sector (companies, professional organizations, interest groups). Party politics, represented by the LDP, presupposed a smooth working of this collaborative system, known as *kanmin-kyōryoku-taisei*. But as described above, this has been continually disrupted by the deterioration of the bureaucratic authority in various ways. To the extent that this authority was derived from the remarkable economic successes of postwar Japan, the financial crises after the bubble burst and the subsequent failure of management have eroded that authority. As the realities of the bureaucratic system were disclosed, the country saw the organization of an independent labyrinthine kingdom for the interests of ex-bureaucrats and their loyal troops.

For example, it has been revealed how the bureaucratic system preyed on the numerous public licensing systems. Japan has 280 national licenses as well as 173 para-national licenses. To oversee the licensing process, the ministries established 73 public service corporations, which proceeded to monopolize and to profit visibly on fees for examinations and recurrent education. These corporations received funds from the ministries for operating costs; they also accepted 229 high-ranking ex-bureaucrats as directors on their boards. The consequence for the now-angry public has been high costs and overregulation. The national licensing system forms only a tiny part of the "hidden empire" of the bureaucratic system, which has been a parasite on the public, more concerned for its own interests than the public interest.

Under the economic stress, the old style of collaborative governance has changed from a plus-sum game to a zero-sum game between the public and private sectors. In some noncompetitive sectors, it worked relatively well, but the worsening of the budget deficit eventually destroyed the preconditions of the collaborative system. Traditionally, local governments were the most loyal partners of the bureaucratic system, but they have become more self-assertive in recent years. Even public works programs have failed to materialize because the local governments have grown alarmed about their own swelling budget deficits. Tokyo Governor Ishihara Shintarō moved to introduce new local taxes despite the passive resistance of bureaucrats, setting an example for other local governments. The central government, represented by the bureaucratic system, has lost power and credibility in relation not only to the global marketplace but also to old partners and the Japanese public.

The paralysis of the old system of governance has required that politicians provide the public with a new system. To the extent that politics is based upon the old, no impressive response has been forthcoming. It is true that Japanese politics has made ostensible efforts to change, but these changes have been too little and too slow.

This inability to act comes at a time that politicians and some members of the populace still think that Japan, as the world's biggest creditor nation, has the luxury of enough money to postpone making tough decisions. The LDP, the party of postwar prosperity, has been passive, unwilling to take the initiative in restructuring the system of governance. In this sense, the LDP is a "conserving" party rather than a "conservative" party. The worst part of a "conserving" politics is that it is responsive to every piecemeal claim and demand with little consideration for responsible policy in the longer term. The 2000 election suggested that Japanese voters have begun to reject this old way of doing business.

The design of the new governance has been proposed by a number of opinion leaders. The report of the Prime Minister's Commission on Japan's Goals in the 21st Century—titled *The Frontier Within: Individual Empowerment and Better Governance in the New Millennium*—presented to Prime Minister Obuchi in 2000 offers one such design. Most proposals recognize that it will be necessary to dismantle the overwhelming presence of bureaucratic power and influence. This power would be more efficiently administered by the market (deregulation) and local governments (decentralization), they say. The tight system of regulation should be replaced by macroeconomic management, removing the closed system of collaboration between bureaucrats and economic actors.

The decentralization of power and resources will give local governments the freedom and responsibility to act according to their own discretion in dealing with concrete issues. Decentralization has been characterized as the most meaningful measure to rectify a highly dependent system as well as to control the irresponsible demands of public works programs by the local community. One result of decentralization is that Diet members will lose the opportunity to win votes by pressing bureaucrats to do something for their constituencies. But another result is that Diet members and the central government can concentrate on providing the rule of law and carrying out an important national agenda, including crisis management. It seems critical for the central government to reestablish its effectiveness by devolving the power of implementation.

From the legal perspective, the reform of the judiciary and the empowerment of the legal profession need also to be pursued. The old governance, represented by authoritarian administrative guidance, should be replaced by legal discussions between equal actors and decisions by the judiciary. The Judicial Reform Council published its comprehensive report in 2001, and among its recommendations were proposals to increase the number of legal professionals licensed each year from one thousand to three thousand, to establish a Japanese-style law school, and to reintroduce the jury system.

Under a new style of governance, the lives of the Japanese will change in many ways. For one, the old style of governance presupposes that every person would belong to a specific organization and remain committed to it for a lifetime. The lifetime employment system has symbolized this relationship. The bureaucracy realized a kind of governance through control of these organizations, either directly or indirectly, through the banking system. While this relationship has long prevailed, lifetime commitment to a specific organization has proven impracticable in the present day, not only because organizations want a more flexible labor market, but also because people want to have more choices regarding how to live. Even young bureaucrats have not been reluctant to leave their ministries to work for private companies or to seek election as candidates for public office. With governance through the control of organizations over, new governance can be established only according to legal formula.

Under the new style of governance, professional groups and nonprofit organizations (NPOs) are likely to exert greater influence. In postgrowth society, many people seem to have turned from the privatized lifestyle of "economic animals" and put their energy into these organizations. Already, the activities of NPOs and voluntary groups have become highly visible in various areas. Ironically, economic crisis and the decline of the lifetime employment system have provided Japanese society with the human resources for the new governance.

In place of the tightly organized, authoritarian system, network-style cooperation seems to be entering the picture. In this paradigm, the university, a relatively non-authoritarian organization in Japanese society, seems to function as an important mediator of social change as well as a center for an intellectual network.

The most serious battlefield of the new governance seems to be the local community, which has been under the extreme pressure of a rapidly aging society. To date, the bureaucracy has proven helpless in the face of this issue, and many Japanese now see new governance at the local level supported by NPOs and other organizations as the most important agenda in the near future.

The new governance can expect interesting changes in the legislative process. Traditionally, bureaucrats have controlled not only the administrative process but also the legislative process, but their influence in the legislative process has waned through the direct participation of various groups in the legislative process. The Japanese political process has become more open than before, a change that has been accelerated by enactment of the Freedom of Information Act in May 1999. While initiatives of the legislative process have moved slowly from the bureaucracy to individual politicians with whom various groups with a legislative agenda try to gain access, now the Diet members have begun to initiate legislation on their own.

Diet members—that is to say, politicians—thus find themselves in the unique position of both actor and designer of the new governance. But are they up to the task? Some skepticism is inevitable, especially as many have been participants in the old governance longer than they have expended energy designing the new one. Observers have noted that the parliamentary system has functioned to maintain the old system and that it may be unable to catch up with the new agenda. The terms in the old political game have been amended. What kinds of pressures can be brought to bear so that real change is effected?

One is urgency. The mushrooming budget deficit demands that the old system be restructured or scrapped. The graying of society will make the old, consensus politics more difficult, as suggested by the election of 2000. Tough decisions in fiscal and tax policy cannot be avoided; when that occurs, the postwar style of governance will have been rendered helpless. For example, it will be politically suicidal to raise taxes without reconsidering the basic relationships between the central and local governments and the restructuring of the "hidden empire" of bureaucrats. The deepening cleavage among the Japanese voters has suggested that radical change would not be out of order. As the economic stress continues unabated, political parties will necessarily reform.

Another is the need for leadership. In the face of drastically changing circumstances, the postwar parliamentary system has produced no real leader. The politics-dominated system is an institutionalized alternative to the bureaucracy-dominated old governance that does not require any constitutional amendment. If Japan is prepared to amend its constitution, one popular proposal is to introduce the direct election of the prime minister by the people. This idea has been endorsed by leading politicians, such as former Prime Minister Nakasone Yasuhiro and DPJ President Hatoyama, and has been supported broadly by the public. According to a news poll, the direct election of the prime minister is now considered the issue with the highest priority for constitutional amendment. Although voters are not certain whom or what kind of prime minister they would like, it is clear they are frustrated with the present shape of the parliamentary system that is managed largely by the LDP. The performance of prime ministers in recent years has been so weak that the call for direct election has grown in strength. The argument for direct election can be bolstered by the fact that prefectural governors are directly elected, and Ishihara in Tokyo and Kitagawa Masayasu in Mie have been effective leaders.

Yet, there are issues to be addressed before any steps are taken. First, it is unclear how the proposal for direct election of the prime minister differs from the parliamentary system or how it is similar to a presidential system. People have been leery of a presidential system in Japan because it echoes the emperor system. Proponents have not put forward a concrete institutional framework, so the real discussion has yet to start. Direct election may overcome some current problems, but it may well introduce some new ones. There is fear among many that the new system would contribute to reestablishing the power of bureaucrats rather than to providing a strong prime minister.

The Real Image of Change

With significant changes in both policy and decision making on slate, how do Diet members feel about this post-postwar situation? What kind of political system do they expect will be realized in the near future?

In October and November of 2000, Diet members were sent a questionnaire; an impressive number (353 of 730) responded. Most of the questions had to do with the substance of the politics-dominated system to be implemented in January 2001. Significantly, 80 percent said that they had a clear image of the new system. When asked to identify that image by the alternative it offered, half the respondents said, "politicians make policy"—an answer supported widely by the DPJ, the LP, and the SDP. On the other hand, 26 percent of Diet respondents indicated the alternative of "governing party makes policy"—an answer most popular among members of the LDP. The third alternative, "prime minister makes policy," was supported by 13 percent, mostly DPJ and New Conservative Party (NCP) members. LDP members liked this alternative image least.

As regards the effectiveness of the new political appointee system, Diet members were not, on the whole, very sanguine about the vice-ministers, although members of the governing parties were relatively positive. When asked whether bureaucrats would be willing to provide vice-ministers and policy advisors with enough information to make policy, 43 percent expressed serious doubt; 25 percent had some doubt. That means 68 percent had doubt about bureaucrats, even as members of the governing parties were relatively optimistic about bureaucratic cooperation.

In response to the question whether vice-ministers and policy advisors would intervene in the administrative system to achieve their special interests and violate the principle of administrative neutrality, opinion was sharply divided. While members of the governing parties were, again, relatively optimistic, 75 percent of respondents saw the reform of political parties as necessary to create an effective politics-dominated system. As a governing actor in Japan, the political party did not have a good reputation. When asked whether stabilizing the term of ministers would help to establish a more effective governing system, an overwhelming majority answered "yes." Only JCP members answered "undecided." As to the question, "Do the bureaucrats lose self-confidence and morale?" 37 percent said "yes"; of these, LDP members outnumbered NK members by 45 percent to 17 percent.

Although the politics-dominated system requires the commitment of Diet members to policymaking, an overwhelming majority of respondents said that they lacked adequate infrastructure to fulfill this role. To the question, "Whose assistance would be the most reliable in policymaking?" the most common answer was the political party and its staff. Second was the Diet member's personal policy staff. Third was bureaucrats. This was followed by the private sector/academics/NPOs and the Diet staff. Diet members belonging to smaller political parties depend on their own party and their staffs, while the support of bureaucrats is still conspicuously important for LDP members. DPJ members depend on party staff, personal staff, the private sector, and the staff of the Diet in relatively equal proportion. Generally speaking, Diet members thought that most of the policymaking support systems, with the exception of the bureaucrats, were inadequate. At the same time, most believed that publicly supported policy staff did not function appropriately.

Finally, regarding the direct election of the prime minister, 76 percent of Diet respondents expressed some interest in the system; 41 percent had relatively strong interest. Thirty-one percent of LDP members had substantial interest, while DP members showed the most interest at 58.9 percent. As might be expected, direct election of the prime minister did not have great appeal to members of smaller parties, but still, as a whole, their interest in the system could be described as remarkable.

When asked what would be the framework for the direct election of the prime minister, almost 30 percent saw it as an institutional change from a parliamentary system to a presidential system, while 51 percent viewed it within the framework of the parliamentary system (see table 3). The responses of the LDP, DPJ, and NK members, in particular, suggested that they had already given some thought to the proposed system.

To the question, "Should the system of the direct election of the prime minister be discussed?" 54 percent of Diet respondents indicated yes, while 30 percent thought it unnecessary (see table 4). For LDP members, the difference between positive and negative responses was not large (42.6 percent versus 38.5 percent). For DPJ and NK members, however, responses were overwhelmingly positive: 73.6 percent versus 12.4 percent for DPJ members and 65.5 percent versus 13.8 percent for NK members. Despite the negative response of the smaller parties, it is clear that Diet members regard the direct election of the prime minister as an issue not easily dismissed.

These results can be interpreted from two aspects. First, the real image Diet members seem to have of the politics-dominated system can be characterized as naive and old-fashioned. It is naive because the underlying issue is not whether politicians should do more in policymaking under the new system, but how they should do it. If they have no concrete answer to the question *how*, the system can be neither revised

Table 3. Institutional Image of the Direct Election of the Prime Minister (%)

	Presidential System	Parliamentary System	Don't Know	Others
Liberal Democratic Party	26.2	51.6	7.4	14.8
Democratic Party	39.5	50.4	3.1	7
New Kōmeitō	24.1	69	0	6.8
Japanese Communist Party	33.3	22.2	11.1	33.3
Social Democratic Party	0	61.1	27.8	11.2
Liberal Party	23.8	33.3	23.8	19
New Conservative Party	16.7	66.7	16.7	0
Others	26.7	53.3	0	20
Independents	25	25	25	25
Total	29.5	51.3	7.4	11.9

Source: Author survey.

Table 4. Should the Direct Election of the Prime Minister Be Discussed? (%)

	Yes	No	Undecided	Don't Know
Liberal Democratic Party	42.6	38.5	18.9	0
Democratic Party of Japan	73.6	12.4	12.4	1.6
New Kōmeitō	65.5	13.8	20.7	0
Japanese Communist Party	0	88.9	11.1	0
Social Democratic Party	33.3	44.4	22.2	0
Liberal Party	14.3	71.4	14.3	0
New Conservative Party	50	50	0	0
Others	73.3	26.7	0	0
Independents	50	25	25	0
Total	54.1	30	15.3	0.6

Source: Author survey.

nor changed. To interpret the new system as the system of domination by the governing party (as was typically represented by LDP members) suggests the old system will continue unchanged. The underlying issue is not whether the governing party should dominate, but *how* it should dominate. In other words, most Diet members still think of the new system in terms of *who* rather than *how*. Understanding a politics-dominated system as meaning a cabinet centered around the prime minister provides the answers to both the questions of *who* and *how*. The new system was established to answer the latter question, not to satisfy party leaders by providing a plethora of new posts. In this sense, Diet members seem not to comprehend the meaning of their responses to the survey.

Diet members find themselves in the unhappy position between the lack of party reform and the poverty of the supporting system. Most of the problems are connected to the *how* and will never be resolved without a systematic, rational approach. The bureaucracy-dominated system has allowed Japanese politics to be occupied with the question of *who*—a legacy that persists even among politicians who supported the end of the bureaucratic system. Without concentrating on *how* to dominate in policymaking, the new system will be stuck with a fragmented bureaucratic system and its haphazard style of decision making.

This lack of comprehension is revealed also in regards to thoughts about the direct election of the prime minister. On one hand, Diet members are reluctant to interpret the politics-dominated system as a prime minister–dominated system; on the other hand, they are sensitive to the public frustration that the present system has failed to provide meaningful political leadership. Some seem to recognize that the present system cannot solve the leadership problem, and so direct election has been considered as a last resort. Israel introduced the direct election of the prime minister because the multiparty system in the Knesset had made the election of the prime minister unwieldy. In Japan, the situation is totally different. The selection of the prime minister and the cabinet has been established.

The real issue in Japan is that the prime minister has been weak within his own party, not vis-à-vis other parties. This intra-party weakness has resulted from a long history of factional politics and the paucity of intra-party cohesion. To address this weakness, some Diet members support direct election within the framework of the parliamentary system. But in this case, there is the attendant issue of how to institutionalize the new parliamentary system. Fundamentally speaking, to introduce direct election to counter intra-party impediments seems asymmetrical. Nor is it clear how far direct election would go toward overcoming intra-party weakness. In the worst-case scenario, it could bring about a weak, personalized politics.

The relatively strong support for the introduction of a presidential system illustrates the desperate perception Diet members may have. The data from the survey point to the decline of the parliamentary system, but it is another matter entirely as to whether a presidential system can solve the difficult *how* questions. If the institutionalized politics-dominated system has provided some answers to the *how* questions, it seems curious that another leap would be made when the result is unpredictable. The direct election proposal offers Diet members the political luxury of answering the *how* question by referring to the *who* question and thus postponing tough decisions.

Postscript

Political changes in 2001—from the resignation of the Mori cabinet and the formation of the cabinet under Prime Minister Koizumi Jun'ichirō to the Upper House election—can be viewed in light of the above discussion. The Koizumi cabinet was formed in a fashion relatively free of the influence of Diet members and party factions, its political base different from that of earlier cabinets. Formed at a time when the public had grown impatient with old-style LDP politics and when the party seemed certain to be defeated in the Upper House, the Koizumi cabinet made its base the broad spread of ordinary voters. It was the de facto breakdown of party politics that made the Koizumi cabinet possible. The cabinet's most striking feature is the extremely high support (over 80 percent) it has enjoyed since its formation, much higher than support for the LDP. Koizumi himself boosted support by stating publicly that he put the reform of Japan before the survival of the LDP. As evidenced by its backing by a large proportion of the opposition DPJ, the Koizumi cabinet is regarded as having transcended the framework of party politics.

The Koizumi cabinet's unique character rests in large part on the prime minister's forthright manner of speech and his skillful use of the media. But the inordinately high support his performance has attracted may be a broader indication of how tired voters had grown with party politics and how much they yearned for a political leader. Thus, Koizumi's popularity is due in larger part to his having liberated the country from "politics as usual" than to his cabinet's policies. Departing from politics as usual, however, does not equate to providing satisfactory policies. It is the latter that will ultimately shape assessment of the cabinet, and the prime minister himself is well aware that his support rate will eventually fall.

The substance of Koizumi's promised reforms will be unveiled in time, but as his cabinet proceeds, it must face the anti-reform group dubbed the "forces of resistance." According to public opinion polls, the biggest such force is the LDP, especially the Hashimoto faction. A situation in which reform by an LDP-based cabinet has as its greatest force of resistance the LDP can only be viewed as paradoxical. The LDP won a convincing victory in the Upper House election, but this was not necessarily the victory of reform forces. Indeed, the fact that an LDP victory would mean an increase in the forces of resistance gave many voters pause, and this is said to have kept the LDP vote from becoming even greater.

The deep tension between the Koizumi cabinet and the LDP may well play itself out if, in the course of reform, the cabinet delivers a blow to vested interests. Cutting back on public works programs, which have nourished the LDP's political base, is unavoidable, and the cabinet's policy to dismantle or privatize public corporations in charge of highway construction will provide a good stress test. These initiatives constitute a direct attack on a domain in which the interests of bureaucrats and LDP Diet policy caucus members converge, and thus are seen as the touchstone of reform. Not only will the forces of resistance seek to hold back reform in individual areas of contention, but they are also sure to push for boosting spending on the grounds that the increased deflationary pressure of reform will slow the economy further. It would suit the LDP perfectly if the parameters of the debate were defined as reform versus economic recovery.

Another focal point is the mechanisms of policymaking. While the establishment of a politics-dominated system is a given, the concrete terms of such a system is the major problem. Prime Minister Mori, in keeping with LDP tradition, took a politics-dominated system to mean a governing party–dominated system and ran his administration accordingly. This approach, however, obscures political leadership and has allowed interest-driven politics by governing-party Diet members to prevail. The Koizumi cabinet has opted for a politics-dominated system that is led by the cabinet and the prime minister. Old style has come up against new style, and the battle has been joined. But if the Koizumi cabinet compromises on this point, it will betray the hopes of the electorate and most certainly lose its political base. The debate over who makes policy decisions, as well as the content of reform, is certain to intensify.

As it is Prime Minister Koizumi who determines when to dissolve the Lower House and to call a general election, he is expected to expose the forces of resistance within the LDP and to apply pressure on them. No doubt, the next general election will be a referendum on the results of reform and the substance of political change. There is no telling whether the Koizumi cabinet, with its difficult intra-party base, can survive until then and, if it does, how party politics will be realigned when the election takes place. What is certain is that it will not be easy to sustain for long the highly paradoxical relationship between the Koizumi cabinet and LDP party politics.

11

The Limits of
Institutional Reform in Japan

R. Kent Weaver

F OR Japan, the last decade has generally been seen as a period of
poor performance and lost opportunities (Lincoln 2001). The
economy has stagnated, and unemployment has risen. In politics
and governance as well, there has been more bad news than good, despite substantial institutional reforms. The new electoral system for the
House of Representatives, instituted in 1994, has succeeded more at creating instability in the party system than it has at ending the system of
factions in the Liberal Domestic Party (LDP) or inducing a system where
strong, competitive parties regularly alternate in office. In addition, Japanese prime ministers have failed to emerge as the kind of leaders able to
steer government to undertake major reforms.

In this atmosphere of profound disappointment, a number of new
proposals for institutional reform have emerged. Electoral reform and
campaign finance reform were both enacted in the early 1990s, and the
idea of the direct election of the prime minister has come to the fore
more recently. Sasaki Takeshi has discussed at length the critical challenges facing governance in Japan amid changing circumstances within
and without. This chapter, in response, draws on international experience as it discusses the capacity of institutional reform to address the
problems that governance in Japan faces.

THE POLITICS OF ELECTORAL REFORM

Arising out of a complex set of factors, the electoral reform of 1994 brought to Japan a mixed-member majoritarian (MMM) electoral system, replacing the single non-transferable vote (SNTV) system (see Curtis 1999, chapter 4; Reed and Thies 2001a, 152–172). MMM was not a first choice. Rather, it emerged as a substantive compromise between the opposing interests of sponsoring parties and the tactical decision of the major parties to support reform so as to avoid the blame of voters for having opposed it (Curtis 1999, 154–157).

In some ways, the new electoral system has corresponded to the expectations of electoral system theorists, if not the proponents of reform. Certainly it shows the emergence of two parties that in size are in a different league from the others. These two parties, the LDP and the Democratic Party of Japan (DPJ) are very large and have many of the attributes of modern "catch-all" parties. That is, they attempt to appeal to median and "free-floating" voters while maintaining support from their core constituencies—for the LDP, rural, older voters and members of the "public works complex"; and for the DPJ, urbanites, younger voters, and public sector unions. The attempt of these parties to appeal broadly to the populace has led to a blurring of their appeal as well: it might be said that the LDP stands for nothing, while the DPJ stands for everything.

As one might expect from an MMM system, however, a constellation of smaller parties continues to exist. In part, this results from the operation of a proportional representation tier, but it has also been facilitated, as in Italy, by the development of electoral alliances in single-seat districts, where one party stands aside in specific districts to facilitate a victory for that seat by a party expected to be their coalition partner after the election. It is too early to tell whether an equilibrium of parties has been reached under the new set of electoral rules—and it is likely that the identity of some parties will undergo a shift over the next few years. But after a period of enormous upheaval in the 1990s, the Japanese party system does seem to be stabilizing somewhat.

It is also too early to tell what will happen to factions within the LDP. The faction system was instituted as a result of intra-party competition sparked by the old system of a single non-transferable vote in small multi-member districts; factions were valuable at providing the financial and organizational support that candidates needed to win in those combined intra- and inter-party contests. A replacement of factions by more unified party branches at the local level was the goal of many proponents of electoral reform in Japan, not least because weakening factions were thought likely to bring about more decisive leadership at the national level. So far, however, the evidence suggests a more complex pattern in which local party branches have been strengthened but factions continue to exist and compete to win the loyalties of new Diet members; at the same time, new Diet members will frequently join factions (see Reed and Thies 2001b, 380–403; Cox, Rosenbluth, and Thies 1999; and Park 2001). They do so because personal support networks continue to serve the interests of legislators. This is evident, for example, in areas where there has been the practice of LDP candidates' alternating between running on a party list and running as a single-seat district candidate as a way to contain conflict between rival LDP politicians. Factions also continue to play a role in allocating top party positions and cabinet posts (see Miyai 2001). It is unlikely that factions will wither away in the near future unless Prime Minister Koizumi Jun'ichirō mounts an all-out campaign against them, and it is unclear whether he could succeed if he tried.

The overall lessons of the Japanese experience are several, and they are humbling for social scientists. First, the consequences of institutional reform are complex, not simple—and they are especially complex for a mixed electoral system like the one that exists in Japan. Second, as Steven Reed and Michael Thies have pointed out (2001b, 380–403), the consequences of institutional reform are path-dependent. They do not appear on a blank slate, but rather in interaction with a set of institutions and interests that are already highly developed. In particular, politicians with substantial resources will try to manipulate a reformed set of institutions to try to maintain their power. Finally, the case of the 1994 reforms shows that the effects of institutional change are not instantaneous; they take some time to shake out. It is far from certain that those changes are over.

DIRECT ELECTION OF THE PRIME MINISTER

Prime Minister Koizumi has proposed the direct election of the prime minister by popular vote as a way to strengthen his power to push reforms and to overcome his dependence on shifting factional and partisan alliances. Koizumi has set up a private advisory panel to study the idea, headed by Professor Sasaki ("Panel Set Up" 2001). This move reflects, in part, disappointment with the results of the 1994 election reform.

Given his position as head of the panel advising the prime minister on direct election, it is understandable that Sasaki has not addressed the merits of that proposal in his chapter. Not being under such constraints myself, it is easy to take a position in opposition to this proposed reform.

Exactly how direct election of the prime minister would work and what its effects would be depend in large measure on the specifics of institutional design: for example, whether the two bodies were elected simultaneously, the conditions under which one or both could force new elections, electoral rules for the Diet, the length of prime ministerial and Diet terms, and whether the prime minister was elected through a plurality or two-round majority election. Simultaneous elections might be expected to minimize ticket splitting between prime ministerial and Diet ballots (although, as will be discussed below, the Israeli experience does not support this supposition) and lessen the probability that the prime minister would face a hostile majority in the Diet. Fixed terms for the prime minister without the ability of the legislature to force new elections weaken the capacity of smaller parties to bring down a prime minister's government, but come closer to an arrangement that is more properly called presidential than parliamentary.

Leaving aside presidential systems, the only country that instituted a system of direct election of prime ministers who remain responsible to the legislature is Israel. The experience was not a happy one. The hope of Israeli political reformers was that direct election of the prime minister would strengthen the chief executive, who would no longer be dependent on the outcome of Knesset elections. Many also thought that it would lead to a stronger role for Israel's two largest political blocs, Labor/Alignment and Likud, as people would vote in Knesset elections according to the parties putting up viable candidates for prime minister (see Rahat 2001, 123–151). The consolidation in party support was in turn expected to make the prime minister less subject to constant threats exerted by small political parties in his coalition.

In fact, however, exactly the opposite happened. The two major parties imploded. People seized the opportunity to vote simultaneously for a prime minister able to command broad support and for a Knesset member representing a much narrower identity or interest. As a result, developing a stable coalition of support became more difficult rather than less, and the bargaining power of smaller parties actually increased (see Hazan 2001, 351–379). In early 2001, the Knesset voted to end direct election of the prime minister.

There is little reason to believe that Japan's experience with direct election of the prime minister would be any more felicitous than was Israel's. Indeed, it could offer a platform for a charismatic leader like Tokyo's popularly elected nationalist governor, Ishihara Shintarō, to win election without close ties to a major party (Parry 2001). And while Japan's MMM electoral system would not lead to the same degree of party fragmentation as in Israel, the probability that a directly elected prime minister would be subject to political blackmail by one or more small coalition partners is high. Given Japan's relatively high barriers to constitutional reform (two-thirds vote in each chamber of the Diet plus a majority in a national referendum), it is unlikely that such a reform could win adoption in any case, especially in the Diet.

There are variants on the direct election model that could make some of the pathologies of the Israeli experience less likely. In particular, opponents of the prime minister could be required to achieve a supermajority rather than a simple majority to trigger new elections. A move to more fixed electoral cycles (see below) could also be useful in lessening the probability of governmental instability if direct election resulted in a more fragmented party system. But as in the case of Japan's electoral reform, the capacity of political elites to adapt new rules to their advantage and the prospect for unanticipated negative consequences should not be underestimated.

Alternative Reforms

If direct election of the prime minister is not likely to be a solution to Japan's governance problems, are their other alternatives that offer more promise? As Sasaki notes in his chapter, "The real issue in Japan is that the prime minister has been weak within his own party, not vis-à-vis other parties." A faction-ridden LDP and a norm of rotation of office to share the spoils of election have inhibited the development of a strong prime minister capable of undertaking bold initiatives that impose short-term costs. International experience suggests a few alternatives that may be helpful in addressing these problems.

The first is to make the leadership selection more independent of party bosses. Koizumi was elected prime minister through a process in which the votes of LDP Diet members and the votes of LDP members in the prefectures were combined. The votes of Diet members were numerically dominant, but the fact that prefectural votes were counted first helped to pave the way for Koizumi's victory. Increasing the weight of popular votes in the selection process would strengthen the role of the party leader even further.

Giving party members a greater say in choosing the party leader is not without its dangers, however. It could lead to a competitive mobilization process by factions and interest groups to enroll members as a means of electing a leader favorable to their interests. Organized interests already weigh heavily in the membership of the LDP—people associated with the construction industry, for example, comprise an estimated 180,000 of the party's 1.36 million members ("New Voting System" 2001).

A second change worth considering is to lengthen the period between elections in order to make it easier for a government to impose policies that cause short-term pain but have some promise of long-term gain. Elections to the two chambers of the Diet are currently not synchronized. Elections to the (lower) House of Representatives take place at least every four years, but can be called by the prime minister more frequently. Elections to the (upper) House of Councillors take place every two years, with half of the chamber up for re-election on each occasion. As a result, the country can be subjected to a national election almost every year—and sometimes more than once in a year. Thus, in the past five years, Japan has endured elections in 1996, 1998, 2000, and 2001. In the Japanese system of frequent rotation of prime ministers and the scapegoating of politicians who lead the LDP into an electoral loss, it is not surprising that party politicians who come into office pledging short-term pain for long-term gain end up delivering neither.

An alternative approach would be to move to fixed quadrennial elections for both chambers with all seats up for election. As in Sweden, earlier general elections could be called by the government, but would not negate the need to hold elections at a fixed date. The incentives to avoid frequent elections in this system are sufficiently high that no early election has been called in Sweden in more than forty years.

A final piece of external advice would be to avoid further changes in the electoral system. There is always the temptation for parties in power to tinker with the electoral system to gain electoral advantage. Already Japan has gone far down that road since the 1994 electoral reform. Changes were made to the proportional representation tier allowing voters to choose an individual candidate rather than the party in that tier (although excess votes convey to the party). This change was brought about during the very low popularity the LDP endured during the tenure of Mori Yoshirō as prime minister. LDP leaders believed that the party would win more votes by attracting star candidates than by appealing to party loyalty.

As in other countries, like Brazil, where this "personalized proportional representation" has been implemented, a contest ensued among the parties to attract wrestlers and other celebrities as candidates (Magnier 2001). The result has been, almost certainly, a corrosive effect on party discipline, as the parties become more dependent on candidates than vice versa. In addition, in 2000, the LDP forced through the Diet cuts in the number of proportional representation seats in the House of Representatives; the representation of smaller parties in that chamber is thus likely to drop (Lincoln 2001, 50).

In summer 2001, there emerged a third reform: the reintroduction of two- or three-member districts for the House of Representatives in some urban areas to replace current single-seat districts. This measure would have almost certainly hurt the DPJ, given its strong urban base. It could have also allowed the LDP's coalition partners—notably the New Kōmeitō—to win additional seats. The move away from single-seat districts in the House of Representatives has for the moment been blocked by opposition from Prime Minister Koizumi, but obviously the temptation to play for gain is still strong ("Reform Plan" 2001; "Coalition Shelves Poll Reform" 2001; "Election Reform" 2001).

Manipulation of electoral micro-rules comes with the potential for serious negative effect, and governing parties would do well to avoid such ploys. First, it undermines voter familiarity with the electoral system that is helpful in voters' making an informed choice. It also risks weakening the legitimacy of the electoral system if it is seen by voters, already cynical enough, as simply another political game where the winners get to split the prize. Third, it can lead to the situation where electoral manipulation for political gain is accepted as a standard rule of the game—a self-reinforcing process with no good or logical end.

The overall lesson, in short, is that formal reform of political institutions should not be seen as a panacea for Japan's many problems. The effects of changes in political institutions are too complex and multifaceted, too unpredictable, and too subject to manipulation by political elites to have any certainty of producing the results intended. Informal changes, such as the relationship between bureaucrats and politicians discussed by Sasaki in his chapter, can play an important role in determining how well Japan is governed.

BIBLIOGRAPHY

"Coalition Shelves Poll Reform for One Year." 2001. *Daily Yomiuri* (1 November): 2.

Cox, Gary, Frances Rosenbluth, and Michael Thies. 1999. "Electoral Reform and the Fate of Factions: The Case of Japan's LDP." *British Journal of Political Science* 29(1): 33–56.

Curtis, Gerald L. 1999. *The Logic of Japanese Politics.* New York: Columbia University Press.

"Election Reform Case of Crossed Wires." 2001. *Daily Yomiuri* (2 November): 3.

Hazan, Reuven Y. 2001. "The Israeli Mixed Electoral System: Unexpected Reciprocal and Cumulative Consequences." In Matthew Soberg Shugart and Martin P. Wattenberg, eds. *Mixed-Member Electoral Systems: The Best of Both Worlds?* New York: Oxford University Press.

Lincoln, Edward. 2001. "Japan in 2000: The Year That Could Have Been But Was Not." *Asian Survey* 41(1): 49–60.

Magnier, Mark. 2001. "In Japan, Celebrity Has Hammerlock on Election." *Los Angeles Times* (28 July): A1.

Miyai Yumiko. 2001. "Disbanding Factions a Daunting Task for Reformist Koizumi." *Daily Yomiuri* (26 April): 17.

"New Voting System Challenges Parties." 2001. *Daily Yomiuri* (19 July): 3.

"Panel Set Up to Discuss Direct Election of Premier." 2001. *Daily Yomiuri* (15 July): 3.

Park Cheol Hee. 2001. "Factional Dynamics in Japan's LDP Since Political Reform: Continuity and Change." *Asian Survey* 41(3): 428–461.

Parry, Richard Lloyd. 2001. "Koizumi Outlines Political Revolution for Japan." *The Independent* (28 April): 15.

Rahat, Gideon. 2001. "The Politics of Reform in Israel: How the Israeli Mixed System Came to Be." In Matthew Soberg Shugart and Martin P. Wattenberg, eds. *Mixed-Member Electoral Systems: The Best of Both Worlds?* New York: Oxford University Press.

Reed, Steven R., and Michael F. Thies. 2001a. "The Causes of Electoral Reform in

Japan." In Matthew Soberg Shugart and Martin P. Wattenberg, eds. *Mixed-Member Electoral Systems: The Best of Both Worlds?* New York: Oxford University Press.

———. 2001b. "The Consequences of Electoral Reform in Japan." In Matthew Soberg Shugart and Martin P. Wattenberg, eds. *Mixed-Member Electoral Systems: The Best of Both Worlds?* New York: Oxford University Press.

"Reform Plan Bald Opportunism." 2001. *Daily Yomiuri* (26 October): 8.

About the Contributors

THOMAS E. MANN is W. Averell Harriman Chair and Senior Fellow in Governmental Studies at the Brookings Institution. Between 1987 and 1999, he was Director of Governmental Studies at Brookings. Before coming to Brookings in 1987, Mann was executive director of the American Political Science Association. Mann earned his B.A. in political science at the University of Florida and his M.A. and Ph.D. at the University of Michigan. His published works include *The Permanent Campaign and Its Future* (2000); *Vital Statistics on Congress* (2002); and *The New Campaign Finance Sourcebook* (2002). He has also written numerous scholarly articles and opinion pieces on various aspects of American politics, including elections, political parties, Congress, the presidency and public policymaking.

SASAKI TAKESHI is President of the University of Tokyo. Upon graduating from the University of Tokyo in 1965, he became Research Associate at the Faculty of Law of the university and was Associate Professor between 1968 and 1978. Sasaki was Visiting Scholar, Fellow of Alexander Humboldt-Stiftung at the University of Erlangen-Nurnberg from 1974 to 1976 and Visiting Scholar, Fellow of American Studies Program at Amherst College from 1981 to 1982. He has been Secretary-General of the Committee for the Promotion of Political Reform since 1992 and was appointed to be a member of the Prime Minister's Commission on Japan's Goals in the 21st Century in March 1999. Sasaki's recent publications include *Seiji kaikaku 1800 nichi no shinjitsu*

(The truth behind 1800 days of political reform, co-edited, 1999); *Purato no jukubaku* (The spell of Plato, 1998); and *Seijika no jōken* (The conditions of politicians, 1995).

E. J. DIONNE JR. is a Senior Fellow in the Governmental Studies Program of the Brookings Institution and a columnist with the *Washington Post*. Before joining the *Post*, Dionne spent 14 years with the *New York Times*. Dionne began his op-ed column for the *Post* in 1993 and has been a regular commentator on politics for CNN and a frequent guest on PBS, NBC, ABC, CBS, and NPR. He joined the Brookings Institution in 1996. Dionne earned his B.A. from Harvard University in 1973 and received his doctorate from Oxford, where he was a Rhodes Scholar. In 1994–1995, he was a guest scholar at the Woodrow Wilson International Center. His publications include *Why Americans Hate Politics* (1991); *They Only Look Dead: Why Progressives Will Dominate the Next Political Era* (1996); and *Community Works: The Revival of Civil Society in America* (editor, 1998).

KATŌ HIDEKI is Representative of Japan Initiative, a nonprofit, policy-oriented think tank that he founded in 1997. He has also been Professor in the Faculty of Policy Management of Keio University since 1997. After graduating from Kyoto University's Faculty of Economics in 1973, he joined the Ministry of Finance, where he assumed various positions including Director at the Minister's Secretariat until he retired from the ministry in 1996. Japan Initiative was established to promote private initiatives in legislative and policy-oriented activities and has been particularly active in facilitating citizens' and NPO's participation in the policy process through proposing a major tax reform and other structural reforms. Katō is the author of several books and articles, including *Min to kan* (The private sector and the public sector, 1999) and *Kinyū shijo to chikyū kankyo* (Financial markets and the global environment, 1997).

PAUL C. LIGHT is Vice President and Director of Governmental Studies at the Brookings Institution, where he is Douglas Dillon Senior Fellow and founding director of the Center for Public Service. He also teaches at Harvard University's John F. Kennedy School of Government. From 1995 to 1998, he was Director of the Public Policy Program at the Pew Charitable Trusts. Light earned his B.A. from Macalester College in 1975 and his M.A. and Ph.D. from the University of Michigan in political science in 1980. Light's publications include *Thickening Government: Federal Hierarchy and the Diffusion of Accountability* (1995); *The Tides of Reform: Making Government Work, 1945–1995* (1998); and *Government's Greatest Achievements: From Civil Rights to Homeland Security* (2002).

JAMES M. LINDSAY is Senior Fellow in the Foreign Policy Studies Program at the Brookings Institution, where he specializes in Congress and foreign affairs, foreign aid, immigration, national missile defense, national security politics, public opinion and foreign affairs, the United Nations, and war powers. Lindsay is former Professor of Political Science at the University of Iowa; former Director for Global Issues and Multilateral Affairs at the National Security Council (1996–1997); and former International Affairs Fellow at the Council on Foreign Relations. He earned his B.A. from the University of Michigan in 1981, his M.A. and M.Phil. from Yale University in 1983, and his Ph.D. from Yale University in 1988. His publications include *Perspectives: Global Issues* (editor, 1998); *Perspectives: World Politics* (editor, 1998); and *Defending America: The Case for Limited National Missile Defense* (2000).

SHIOZAKI YASUHISA is a Liberal Democratic Party (LDP) Member of the House of Representatives and a former Parliamentary Vice Minister of Finance (1997–1998). After graduating from the University of Tokyo in 1975, he entered the Bank of Japan. He was elected to the House of Representatives in 1993, to the House of Councillors in 1995, and to the House of Representatives for the second time in 2000. He is currently Director of the Committee on Judicial Affairs, House of Representatives. His posts in the LDP include Acting Chairman, Social Affairs and Labor Division, Policy Research Council; Secretary-General, Administrative Reform Headquarters; Chairman, Sub-Committee on International NGOs; Chairman, Sub-Committee on Corporate Accounting; and Deputy Director, Research Commission on the Tax System, Policy Research Council. He received his M.A. in public administration from the John F. Kennedy School of Government at Harvard University in 1982.

TANIGUCHI MASAKI has been Associate Professor of Japanese Politics, Graduate School of Law and Politics, University of Tokyo since 1996. Upon graduating from the University of Tokyo in 1993, he became Research Associate of the Graduate School of Law and Politics, University of Tokyo. Taniguchi's publications include *Nihon no taibei bōeki kōshō* (The U.S.-Japan trade relationship: Its structure and transfiguration, 1997); "Mittsu no saifu wo tsukaiwakeru daigishi" (MPs' three wallets, *Asahi Sōken Report*, No. 36, 1999); *Daigishi to kane* (Diet members and money, co-edited, 1999); and *Seiji kaikaku 1800 nichi no shinjitsu* (The truth behind 1800 days of political reform, co-edited, forthcoming).

R. KENT WEAVER has been a Senior Fellow in the Governmental Studies Program at the Brookings Institution since 1987. He is also Adjunct Professor at the Nitze School of Advanced International Studies of Johns Hopkins University. His major fields of interest and expertise are American and comparative social policy, comparative political institutions, Canadian politics, and the politics of expertise. Weaver is the author of *Ending Welfare As We Know It* (2000), *Automatic Government: The Politics of Indexation* (1988), and *The Politics of Industrial Change* (1985). He is the co-author and editor of *The Collapse of Canada?* (1992) and co-author and co-editor of *Looking Before We Leap: Social Science and Welfare Reform* (1995), *Do Institutions Matter?: Government Capabilities in the U.S. and Abroad* (1993), and *Think Tanks and Civil Societies* (2000). Weaver graduated from Haverford College and received his M.A. and Ph.D. in political science from Harvard University.

YOSHIDA SHIN'ICHI has been Editor of News Projects and Opinion at the *Asahi Shimbun* since 2000 and Visiting Professor at the University of Tokyo since 1997. He joined the *Asahi Shimbun* in 1974, and as a member of the Politics Department has concentrated on Japanese and American politics. As a staff journalist and later a senior reporter, he has reported on the Liberal Democratic Party, with specific attention on the Tanaka faction. During the 1990s, he served as a Guest Reporter-at-Large for th*e Boston Globe*, Political Correspondent at the *Asahi Shimbun's* Washington General Bureau (1991–1994), and Chief Correspondent for the Prime Minister's Office. He received the Japan Newspaper Publishers' and Editors' Association Award (the Japanese equivalent of the Pulitzer Prize) in 1978 and 1996, and the Japan Congress of Journalists' Prize in 1978. Yoshida holds a B.A. in law from the University of Tokyo, and an M.P.A. from the Kennedy School of Government, Harvard University.

Index

Japan Center for
International Exchange

FOUNDED in 1970, the Japan Center for International Exchange (JCIE) is an independent, nonprofit, and nonpartisan organization dedicated to strengthening Japan's role in international affairs. JCIE believes that Japan faces a major challenge in augmenting its positive contributions to the international community, in keeping with its position as one of the world's largest industrial democracies. Operating in a country where policymaking has traditionally been dominated by the government bureaucracy, JCIE has played an important role in broadening debate on Japan's international responsibilities by conducting international and cross-sectional programs of exchange, research, and discussion.

JCIE creates opportunities for informed policy discussions; it does not take policy positions. JCIE programs are carried out with the collaboration and cosponsorship of many organizations. The contacts developed through these working relationships are crucial to JCIE's efforts to increase the number of Japanese from the private sector engaged in meaningful policy research and dialogue with overseas counterparts. JCIE receives no government subsidies; rather, funding comes from private foundation grants, corporate contributions, and contracts.